With Him in Life's Struggles

Discovery House Publishers

Books, music, and videos that feed the soul with the Word of God

Box 3566 Grand Rapids, MI 49501

With Him in Life's Struggles

A Woman's Study on the Faithfulness of God From 2 Samuel

Myrna Alexander

With Him in Life's Struggles
Copyright © 1994 by Myrna Alexander

Discovery House books are distributed to the trade exclusively by
Barbour Publishing, Inc., Uhrichsville, Ohio 44683.

Unless otherwise indicated, Scripture is taken from the
HOLY BIBLE, NEW INTERNATIONAL VERSION.
Copyright © 1973, 1978, 1984 International Bible Society.
Used by permission of Zondervan Bible Publishers.

Library of Congress Cataloging-in-Publication Data

Alexander, Myrna.
With Him in life's struggles / Myrna Alexander
p.   cm.

ISBN 0-929239-92-X

1. Bible. O.T. 2 Samuel—Study and teaching. I. Title.
BS1467.A44 1992   223'.70076—dc20   95-5466
CIP

Discovery House Publishers is affiliated with
RBC Ministries, Grand Rapids, Michigan 49512

Printed in the United States of America

06 08 10 11 09 07 05
CHG
7 9 11 13 14 12 10 8

To my Mother and Father
who created in their children
a desire to know God.

Other books by
Myrna Alexander

Woman of Wisdom: Lessons for Living
from the Book of Proverbs
Discovery House Publishers

Behold Your God: A Woman's Workshop
on the Attributes of God
Zondervan Publishing House

Loving and Obeying God: A Woman's Workshop
on 1 Samuel
Zondervan Publishing House

Contents

Acknowledgments   8

Preface   9

How To Use This Bible Study   12

Suggestions for Leaders   13

Lesson 1   The God Who Is With Us   15

Lesson 2   Waiting on God Is Never a Waste of Time   25

Lesson 3   God's Way Is Effective   33

Lesson 4   God's Plan Is Great   43

Lesson 5   The Alternative to Hopelessness   51

Lesson 6   The Turning Point   61

Lesson 7   Consequences—The Chain Reaction   71

Lesson 8   The Betrayal and the Support   77

Lesson 9   How To Stand When You've Been Flattened   87

Lesson 10   "Oh No, Not a New Problem!"   95

Lesson 11   Song of Thanksgiving   103

Lesson 12   A Morning Without Clouds   111

Lesson 13   The Charge   121

Acknowledgments

For God's work to be done effectively, a variety of His people and their various gifts are needed. "To each one the manifestation of the spirit is given for the common good" (1 Corinthians 12:7). Few works for God are achieved single-handedly: His work is accomplished when the parts of Christ's body work together.

With Him in Life's Struggles illustrates well this principle because it is the result of God at work through His people.

I am thankful for the women in our weekly Women's Bible Study that originally studied this material on 2 Samuel. I am especially grateful for Doris, Lynn, Jan, Carolyn, Jeanie, Julie, Kay, Rosemary, Carol, and Olga, who were committed to meet every Tuesday morning for training and prayer in preparation for our Thursday Women's Study. Their interaction proved invaluable to me.

Special appreciation goes to my faithful friend, Ginni Montague-Rock, Professor of English Literature at the University of Vienna, who eagerly reviewed each lesson and offered many wise insights.

I am exceedingly grateful for the dedication, faithfulness, and God-given expertise of my dear friend and typist Sylvia Jones without whom these lessons would never have arrived at the publisher.

Once again I am deeply appreciative of my husband's encouragement and biblical counsel, as well as for the specific prayer support of my family, friends, and church family.

Preface

"I have chosen the way of truth; I have set my heart on your laws" (Psalm 119:30).

In the spring and summer of 1994 I had a fascinating, time-machine type experience. Through the printed page I was transported back ten years while revising the Bible study book on 2 Samuel I wrote in 1984. Reading through my earlier examination and application of the study gave me a chance to see the results of the biblical content in my life, and that of my family. I made an important observation: I discovered that whether one is a child or an adult, ten years has eternal significance when the commitment described in the above verse has been made.

The following conversation, recorded in my original preface, took place ten years ago.

"My eleven year old daughter, Christina, came bouncing into the room where I sat staring at a sheet of paper on my desk entitled, 'Study Summary of 1 and 2 Samuel.' "

"Christina," I suddenly asked, "what do you think it means to be a person after God's heart?"

She was silent for a moment and then quietly said, "It means loving God."

I was struck by her answer. She had said so clearly what had taken me so long to begin to see.

"Well, what does it mean to love Him?" I pursued.

"It means talking to Him, reading His Word, and wanting to do what He says," she summarized simply.

Wanting to continue our conversation, I quickly added, "What difference do you think it would make in a girl's life if she loved God?"

"She would be happier," she said broadly smiling.

"Then why don't we all love God?" I responded.

"Because we think that we can make ourselves happy by getting what we want. Everybody thinks they are so busy that they don't have time to talk to God and read the Bible. I guess people are too busy to love God."

I sat there looking at her, wondering if she realized the significance of what she was saying and reflecting about God's working in both of our lives. Could it be, I marveled, that these past years of study in 1 and 2 Samuel had so affected my life that it was in turn also affecting hers. I prayed that it was true and that it would lead her to commitment to God and His ways.

The summer of 1994 I stood at the bedroom doorway silently watching my twenty-one-year-old daughter, Christina, as she pored over the books on her desk. She had submerged herself in the pursuit of relating biblical truth to her academic studies as she prepared for her senior year in college. The motivating desire of her research was that her friends realize that God is truth. Observing her intensity, I reflected upon the recently reread conversation she and I had shared ten years ago. I realized that she is now living out her commitment to God and His Word. Loving God, she is obeying Him, becoming a woman after His heart.

In 1 and 2 Samuel the concept of love for God that is emphasized is not one of words but of commitment. It is out of a commitment to God and His Word that one obeys God. This commitment to walk in God's ways is seen as the only route to godly success.

Our present age is characterized by compromise and lack of commitment. Therefore, we once again need to hear the call made in 1 and 2 Samuel to be after God's heart.

In 2 Samuel we discover real people who are struggling with how to love God in their everyday lives. King David illustrates this struggle in his role as leader, parent, and friend. Learning what it is to love and obey God takes place in a setting very much like our own. Reading

2 Samuel is like reading today's morning newspaper. Issues of incest, rape, adultery, murder, deception, pride, parental modeling, the result of not dealing with sin, and the overindulgence of children are in the narrative. The life situations of 2 Samuel are contemporary and instructive for those with "ears to hear." It is within this context that the 1 and 2 Samuel challenge is given: Anyone who commits herself to loving God will become a person after God's heart.

It is my earnest prayer that this study of 2 Samuel will encourage all who use it to be motivated and enabled within the struggles of life to become one after God's heart.

How To Use This Bible Study

With Him in Life's Struggles was originally written for women who wanted to study the Bible together as a group *after* having studied a passage on their own during the week. I believe individual study is the key to a group Bible study whose goal is to see lives changed. Growth and encouragement took place in our group because we came together prepared and with open minds and hearts to God's Word.

Effective study of the Bible involves commitment. Consequently this study guide requires consistent and serious study. The lessons are intended to be done on a regular basis; one discovery section per day, one lesson per week. The approximate time of study for each Daily Discovery is 15 to 20 minutes. There is, however, room for flexibility according to the needs of the individual or group using the material. The result of the work is fruitful and life-changing group discussions.

Finally, it is my prayer that each person who uses these studies will experience the joy and growth that comes from daily studying God's Word.

Suggestions for Leaders

The leader's primary goal is not to teach but to lead a discussion in which the participants feel free to share discoveries from their private study of the Bible. A wise leader can encourage learning by:

1. Trusting the Holy Spirit to work through her.

2. Providing a warm atmosphere in which all are encouraged to participate.

3. Keeping the discussion "on track." The discussion should not be based on what people think but on what God's Word says. The lesson questions are designed to enable this. The leader can always ask, "How did you answer the next question?"

4. Attempting to cover all the assigned passages and questions. This encourages the participants to finish the study.

5. Maintaining this rule: Only those who have finished the week's assignment may share in the discussion. What better way to encourage study?

6. Shortening or rephrasing the questions, when necessary, for the sake of time or interest.

7. Varying the method. Some questions will lend themselves to discussion. Sometimes observations from several women may broaden the group's understanding; at other times, an answer from one person may be sufficient.

8. Summarizing the lesson. Some groups like the leader to summarize the lesson. A summary should give both the biblical principles found in the passages (see the "Key Principles" section at the end of each lesson) and the applications that specifically relate to the group's needs.

Lesson 1

The God Who Is With Us

The two of us were traveling by car through the narrow back streets of Vienna, Austria, where we live. As I drove, I listened carefully to my friend, Carolyn, as she reflected on the ways God has prepared her for her role as president of a large international women's organization.

"I grew up in a rural community in Washington state," she shared. "How could I have known that the circumstances I was facing there would be part of the training for what I'm doing today? For example, several family members faced severe rejection because of mental and physical disabilities. Dealing with this pain together as a family taught me much about handling limitations with sensitivity. This knowledge has been invaluable as I seek to help our multifaceted organization reach out constructively to the needs of others. There have been many other 'training grounds' since. Some of my experiences I called 'good,' others 'bad.' Now I'm beginning to see that He has been in control of it all. I am learning 'as for God, His way is perfect' " (Psalm 18:30).

David the shepherd boy, who became Israel's great king, made this same discovery 3000 years ago. God promised David that he would be the next king of Israel many years before David was actually proclaimed king by his countrymen. David struggled to picture God's promise taking place while he lived the life of an exiled fugitive, hunted as an outlaw by his countrymen. It hardly seemed the route to the throne for David to be fleeing from the very nation God had called him to lead. Yet as

2 Samuel begins, David the fugitive becomes David the king as he is anointed ruler over the house of Judah. Second Samuel demonstrates God's faithfulness to David. Even a brief overview of the book reveals God at work in the seemingly confusing details of David's life. None of David's training was wasted and no experience was unnecessary.

This is an encouragement to me. At times I too struggle to believe that certain promises of God will come true in my life. It is hard to see God at work when I am enmeshed in a trying life circumstance.

One such time I prayed earnestly for my husband to be helped in a large ministry project he had been given. We knew he should be doing this work, but we knew he could not do it alone. "My God shall supply all our need . . ." (Philippians 4:19), we read. Instead of focusing on God, I began to "picture" the various ways God could supply our need. My eyes strained to the horizon watching for the help to come. I became so focused on the way I thought God would help my husband, that I missed what God was actually doing. For God was answering our need among the young men who were already involved in the project with us.

Often I remind myself that like David, I may find I am forced to be on a road that appears to go off at a tangent from God's purposes. Yet, our ways are not God's ways. As we will see in this lesson, God is in control and His purposes will be accomplished. The God who was with David wherever he went, the God who trained my friend Carolyn to be a wise president, is the God who is with me.

The training of David in 1 Samuel proves effective as we enter into 2 Samuel with David as king. As we begin our study of 2 Samuel, there are two key aspects to grasp that will help us understand the message of the book. First, we need to see the historical context and preparation of David to be king. Second, it is important to get an overview, or the big picture, of the book as a whole. This is the purpose of the first lesson.

Understanding the Historical Setting of
1 and 2 Samuel

The nation of Israel is at one of its lowest points as 1 Samuel begins. Religiously and militarily Israel is falling apart. The priesthood is decadent and Israel's enemies, the Philistines, are victorious over them. God characterized His people in this way: ". . . everyone did as he saw fit" (Judges 21:25). It was a time of religious and political anarchy. A time where people followed their own hearts and not God's. A time of willfulness and disobedience. How did Israel get to this point?

Moses led God's people from Egypt to the edge of the land that God had promised to Abraham and his descendants. Then Moses' disciple and successor, Joshua, led Israel into the land. This new period in Israel's history began triumphantly. Here was a new generation of Israelites. They had learned from their fathers' tragic mistake of unbelief. Now the offspring of those who had failed in the wilderness wanderings believed that God would use them to conquer Canaan for their homeland. Victoriously, they began to take the land in the name of the Lord. But in time these same Israelites made a devastating error with disastrous results: they did not fully carry out God's clear commands to drive the pagan inhabitants from the land! This disobedience became a cancer, destroying the nation's spiritual vigor. Instead of Israel being a witness to those around her, she began to accept what God had condemned.

Eventually the Israelites who had worshiped God forsook His ways entirely. God warned Israel that He could not bless disobedience. Loving His people, He disciplined them so they would return to Him and the blessing of His good ways. This discipline came in the form of oppression as God used foreign nations to correct His people. Many nations bordering Israel began to move in on her, first as irritants, and later as destroyers. When the situation became unbearable, the people cried out to God in desperation. They repented in humility and began to walk in God's ways. But soon the pagan influences enticed them again. This became a recurring cycle of sin, sorrow, supplication, salvation, and then sin again. The continuous repetition of this cycle obviously weakened the people's love for God and respect for His authority until ". . . everyone did as he saw fit" (Judges 21:25). This graphic summary concludes the book of Judges, providing the immediate background to 1 and 2 Samuel.

As the book of Samuel opens, a new period begins in Israel's history. Israel is at one of her lowest points. However, the struggling Israelites overlooked their disobedience to God and began to attribute their many problems to the fact they did not have a king. The people insisted on having a king like the nations around them. God gave them what they wanted, but He warned His people about the results of their choice (1 Samuel 8). Israel's government was designed to be a theocracy with God as the ruler; now Israel desired a monarchy with a man as the ruler. Thus, God's people were choosing to move from being ruled by God, whom they could not see, to being ruled by a person whom they could see. The people no longer wanted to trust God alone. It was too hard to believe God would raise up new leaders. God warned Israel about the dangers of a monarchy, yet in His mercy, He provided a way in which the new monarchy could operate successfully and be blessed.

If Israel's king submitted himself to God's leadership, fully carrying out God's directives, God would work His will through him. The responsibility of the king was to administer the covenant God made with Israel at Sinai, submitting himself to the heavenly King. Alongside the king was the role of prophet of God whose task was to interpret the covenant's commands. The responsibilities of king and prophet were to go hand in hand in the new monarchy. A divinely led monarchy was the same as a theocracy except there was now another link in the chain. This was the underlying concept when the last Judge of Israel, Samuel, who also was a priest, anointed the first king of Israel. First Samuel records Israel's history during the transition period from the judges to the beginning of the monarchy. This establishment of the kingdom from a loosely connected group of tribes to a consolidated kingdom under David, is a central theme in 1 and 2 Samuel.

Unfortunately, Israel's first king, Saul, missed the point of how a divinely led monarchy was to function. Saul failed to carry out fully the commands of his heavenly King. Saul compromised, doing what was right in his own eyes (1 Samuel 15:13–23). First Chronicles 10:13–14 records this revealing epitaph: "Saul died because he was unfaithful to the LORD; he did not keep the word of the LORD and even consulted a medium for guidance, and did not inquire of the LORD."

After Saul's failure to obey, God looked for a man after His heart and chose David as the next king of Israel. David understood the proper concept of a monarchy. He knew he was the visible representative of God, carrying out God's directives. This characterized David's rule and may, in part, have been why David was known as a man after God's heart. As David carried out his role as human king, fulfilling the instructions of the heavenly King, there was blessing for David and the nation (2 Samuel 6:11–15, 17–19; especially 7:27–29). However, when he or his descendants deliberately disobeyed, he (and later they) experienced God's discipline.

Second Samuel is the history of David's reign as king of Israel. David was first crowned king over Judah and then over the whole nation. During the reigns of both Saul and David, God brought the separate, loosely knit tribes to see their desperate need to unify in order to stand against their enemies. David, under the guidance of the Spirit of God, consolidated the nation. Under his spirit-led rule Israel became a great nation, and during

Lesson 1: *The God Who Is With Us*

the reign of David—and later under his son Solomon—Israel experienced its golden age.

For most of the period covered in 1 and 2 Samuel there was a political vacuum on the international scene with no major ruling power. All the ancient empires were either at a weak point or had passed into insignificance. The pharaohs of Egypt were weak and in conflict with the religious priesthood who also wanted to rule. The decline of the once powerful Hittites made them no longer a threat. David defeated the Philistines so that they never again rose to power. Only the Aramean tribes to the north posed any possible resistance to the united kingdom under David. Therefore, Israel was able to develop as a nation without external pressures.

Who Wrote 2 Samuel and When?

The author, or authors, who wrote the books of Samuel are unknown. The biblical text makes no specific mention of the author even though 1 Samuel 10:25 indicates some written records were made by Samuel. In 1 Chronicles 29:29 we read about records of David's reign written by Samuel, Nathan, and Gad. Perhaps it is on the basis of this verse that Jewish tradition claims that Samuel wrote the first part of the book until his death, followed by Nathan and Gad who supplied additional information after Samuel died. Most likely the records of Samuel, Nathan, and Gad were used by an inspired historian or editor who compiled the books under the sovereign direction of the Spirit of God.

When did the composition of the books of Samuel take place? The compiling of records and writing of the narrative could not have been finished before David's death in about 970 B.C., since 2 Samuel 23:1 records the last words of David. Therefore, most scholars put the date of the composition of the Samuel books somewhere between the death of David and the Assyrian captivity in 722 B.C.

Getting the Big Picture

This introductory lesson is significant for it sets the stage for the book. It is like the libretto at the opera. My husband and I went to see *La Traviata.* We were thankful to have read the libretto, or storyline, of the opera prior to the performance because it prepared us to understand and enjoy the work.

In the same way, when you and I study a book of the Bible, we first need to see the big picture. Each biblical book was originally read as a whole, not slowly dissected a verse at a time. We need to see the whole or we will not understand the parts correctly. In an overview we don't focus on the details of the story. It is not the story alone we want to focus on, but the message that comes through the narrative. We discover what is happening. As major themes reoccur we begin to see why it is happening. An overview is exciting because we see what God is getting at. Main concepts that God is seeking to reveal for the benefit of future generations begin to surface.

Finally, it is important to see how all the chapters in the book relate to one another. How do they fit together? What is God doing in history at each point? When you read through 2 Samuel this week, ask yourself this question: What is the message here and how is it revealed?

Study Lesson 1

Daily Discovery I

As you begin to read through 2 Samuel, commit your time to the Lord, according to the challenge of Proverbs 16:3: "Commit to the LORD whatever you do, and your plans will succeed."

1. Read 2 Samuel 1–4. In two or three sentences summarize what is happening and why.

2.   What is the basic message of these chapters?

3.   In what ways might this message relate to your life?

Daily Discovery II

Ask God to enable you to understand what you read. "The unfolding of your words gives light; it gives understanding to the simple" (Psalm 119:130).

4.   Read 2 Samuel 5–10.
5.   How does this section relate to the one before it?

6.   Can you see any themes surfacing in the progressive development of the book to this point? If so, what are they?

Daily Discovery III

Today make Psalm 119:133 your personal prayer: "Direct my footsteps according to your word; let no sin rule over me."

7.   Read 2 Samuel 11–14.
8.   Chapter 11 introduces the turning point in David's career. What is the core of it?

9.   What warning to your own life do you see here?

10. Since we are discovering the flow of the book, relate these chapters to the ones before them.

Daily Discovery IV

"Trouble and distress have come upon me, but your commands are my delight" (Psalm 119:143). Commit your reading to the Lord.

11. The literal outworking of this statement in Psalm 119:143, in light of the events recorded in 2 Samuel 15, is found in David's personal words written while he was fleeing from his son Absalom.

    a.   Read Psalm 63.

    b.   In light of the circumstances David faced in 2 Samuel 15, how is the message in this psalm a help to you?

12. Briefly relate these chapters to the ones before them.

Daily Discovery V

"Great peace have they who love your law, and nothing can make them stumble" (Psalm 119:165).

13. Read 2 Samuel 20–24.

14. Write out your own summary statement of the book. Be sure to incorporate the main concepts you discovered in the various sections of 2 Samuel.

15. David is referred to in the Scripture as a person with a heart after God. After reading through 2 Samuel, what do you think it means to have a "heart after God?"

In personal response to the message of 2 Samuel, name a specific action you need to take.

Lesson 2

Waiting on God Is Never a Waste of Time

Memory Verse: "Wait for the LORD; be strong and take heart and wait for the LORD" (Psalm 27:14).

Seven years teaching in Eastern Europe enabled me to see it first hand. When the Iron Curtain came down, there was euphoria. For the Christians in Eastern Europe there was great thanksgiving and praise to God. It had been so hard for so long. Under communism, Christians were persecuted, oppressed, tortured, and killed. Difficult years went on and on like a long dark tunnel going nowhere. But Christians waited on God, strengthened themselves in the Lord, and ministered to others.

Then suddenly, unexpectedly, there seemed a brilliant light in the tunnel. The communist governments fell. The people were free. It's over, the Christians thought. "Now we can really minister, and the purposes of God can be accomplished in a big way," they said. But when the rejoicing was over, many found one hard thing had been replaced by another. As one woman told me in tears, "We thought we were out of the tunnel. We thought it would be so much better, but we never pictured this! Empty shop windows are now full of products no one can buy. Food, medicine, and technical equipment from the West is siphoned off to be sold on the black market. Even within the Christian community many are vying for positions that provide the opportunity to put themselves, or their individual ministries, forward at the cost of others."

Nothing seems harder than coming to the end of a difficult time and finding it is not the end. The trying situation is almost over, but not quite. When sticking to God's way means waiting longer, it is tempting to take things into our own hands. "I can't wait any longer! I won't wait. I'm going to do something about it now," our heart cries out.

David could have said, "This is it! I have waited for years on God in my difficult circumstances. Now that those awful years of being hated, hunted, and forced to hide are over, I'm taking what is rightfully mine!" Now that Saul was dead, why shouldn't David go ahead and claim by force what rightfully belonged to him? Had not God anointed David to be the next king of Israel (1 Samuel 16:12–13)?

It must have been hard for David when the path to the throne was once more blurred as civil war broke out in the fragmented nation of Israel. The people of Judah made David their king but the rest of the tribes stayed loyal to the house of Saul. To encourage this loyalty, Abner, Saul's nephew and the army's commander-in-chief, saw to it that Saul's son Ish-Bosheth was crowned king.

In spite of what may have seemed a slow timetable and a disappointing route, David humbly accepted what God allowed in his life. Through the training years, David had gained understanding concerning the character of his God and declared, "As for God, His way is perfect" (Psalm 18:30).

Cultural Insights

The Cities of Hebron: After Saul's death, God directed David to the cities of Hebron (2 Samuel 2:1). *Hebron* means brotherhood and the group of cities known as "Hebron" served as the center of the confederation of families that made up Judah. Hebron, in the famous vineyard region about twenty miles south of Jerusalem, was the oldest city in the land. How appropriate that David should be crowned king in this ancient city in which Abraham, Isaac, Jacob, and Joseph were buried.

Polygamy: In David's time, political strength was increased through alliances that were sealed by marriage. Such treaties resulted in polygamy. Harems, therefore, were part of court life. God's ideal for marriage was monogamy (compare Genesis 2). Though polygamy was the accepted custom in the nations around Israel, God only tolerated polygamy in Old Testament times because of the hardness of Israel's heart and that of the king. Polygamy always brought trouble to those involved (see 1 Samuel 1, for example). Along with having many wives, kings commonly kept mistresses or concubines. However, there were clear instructions for Israel's king in Deuteronomy 17:15–17 including the command not to take many wives. Usurping the harem of the king or to "lie with" a king's concubine was tantamount to taking the king's place.

Study Lesson 2

Daily Discovery I **David, King of Judah**

1. a.   Read 2 Samuel 2:1–11.

b.   How did David determine what he should do after King Saul's death (2 Samuel 2:1)? What does this first say about David as a person and then about his leadership?

c.   How is God's faithfulness to David demonstrated in 2 Samuel 2:1–4? (See also 1 Samuel 16:1–13.)

d.   Are you unsure of how to respond to an issue in your life? What specifically have you done about it? In what ways does 2 Samuel 2:1–4 encourage you?

2. What does David's first act as king of Judah reveal about his character (2 Samuel 2:4–7)?

3. a. Why do you think Abner wanted Ish-Bosheth as king and not David (2 Samuel 2:8–10; see also 2 Samuel 3:6–11)?

b. Can you think of situations in which this same thinking occurs today?

c. Convicted by his own words, what did Abner know about the one who was to be the next king of Israel (2 Samuel 3:9–10, 17–18)? If Abner already knew God's will, why do you think he had not responded to it before now? What does this say to you personally?

4. David knew that he had been anointed by God to rule over the whole nation (see 1 Samuel 16), yet he did not try to stop Saul's son from being crowned king. What does this indicate about David?

Daily Discovery II **Civil war begins in Israel**

5. a. Read 2 Samuel 2 and 3.

b. Who initiated the terrible contest between King David's men and those of King Ish-Bosheth (2 Samuel 2:12–14)?

c. Observing the text carefully, summarize 2 Samuel 2: 17–32 as if for a News Brief.

6. a. What conclusion can you make about the outcome of the day's sad events (2 Samuel 2:15–28)?

b. In what ways was this first battle prophetic in light of 2 Samuel 3:1?

7. a. What do you learn about God and His ways by comparing 1 Samuel 16:1, 12–13 with what happened fifteen years later in 2 Samuel 2–3?

b. How does this account encourage you today? Be specific.

Daily Discovery III and IV   **The civil war ends**

8. a. In 2 Samuel 3:2–5 the status of David's growing family is mentioned without commentary. According to Deuteronomy 17:15–18, what guidelines were given to the king of Israel? List

God's reason (if stated) for a particular guideline.

b. What do these guidelines indicate about human nature? What do they teach us about God? Consider David's actions in 2 Samuel 3:2–5, 14, and 5:13 in light of Deuteronomy 17:15–18. What does this reveal about David?

c. Can you think of an area in which believers today commonly break a specific command of God by following a culturally acceptable practice? Is there an area in your life in which you may be doing this?

9. Describe King Ish-Bosheth (2 Samuel 2:8–10; 3:7–11; 4:1). In whom or what did Ish-Bosheth place his faith? What was the result of this choice?

10. God anointed David to be king of Israel a long time before the actual event occurred. For years, David had to trust God to carry out His plan in His way. As David waits, what significant event takes place in the sovereign working of God (2 Samuel 3:8–10, 17–19)?

11. Compare David's response to Abner (2 Samuel 3:20–23) with that of Joab (2 Samuel 3:22–30). What biblical principle did Joab break? (See also Deuteronomy 32:43; Romans 12:19–21.)

12. Why did King David demand the response of 2 Samuel 3:31–37? Consider the result David's action had on the nation as a whole (see 2 Samuel 3:36–37).

13. What plan of action did David choose when he didn't know how to deal with the sons of Zeruiah (2 Samuel 3:38–39)?

Daily Discovery V   **Ish-Bosheth's murder**

14. a.   Read 2 Samuel 4.
    b.   What were the motives behind the actions of Baanah and Recab?

    c.   What did these men not know or remember about David? (Compare 2 Samuel 1:1–16 with 2 Samuel 4.)

15. What principle from this chapter might relate to a characteristic of a person after God's heart?

Key Principles from Lesson 2

1.   The first step in making plans is to ask the Lord (2 Samuel 2:1).

2.   Waiting on God is not a waste of time (2 Samuel 1).

3.   Take time to let others know you appreciate their good works (2 Samuel 2:1–7).

4.   Do not rely on human ways to achieve God's goals (2 Samuel 2:8–11).

5.   The warnings of Scripture have a purpose; ignoring them is dangerous (2 Samuel 3:2–5; Deuteronomy 17:15–17).

6.   Trust in God alone, not other people (2 Samuel 4:1).

7.   God can cause someone who is against us to be for us (2 Samuel 3:9–10, 17–18).

8.   Destroying others for personal gain is a sin and will be punished (2 Samuel 4).

Lesson 3

God's Way Is Effective

I hate to wait in the market line, in a waiting room, on a narrow street behind a huge turning truck, for the grass to grow, for the house to sell, for the situation to work out. Waiting seems such a waste of time. I can hardly believe that God would allow, let alone plan, such an activity. Yet how limited is my perspective! Scripture declares the truth, "As for God, *His* way is perfect (Psalm 18:30, italics added). "Blessed are all who wait for Him" (Isaiah 30:18).

But waiting is not only frustrating, at times it is painful. How can that be perfect? I saw this graphically illustrated recently.

In our village lives a pediatrician from Canada. When she made the decision to follow her husband to his new job in Austria, she thought it was right. She gave up her prestigious medical practice, her lovely home, her expensive car, her personal license plates, her new furniture, her important friends, and her notable reputation. She found herself alone in a house with lots of dust, a baby, a toddler, no friends, no family, no car, no self-esteem, and a body so racked with pneumonia she couldn't even walk to the local store. No one appreciated her sacrifice. "How could this be right?" she asked herself.

There was nowhere to go; she had no choice but to wait. "I felt I was waiting in an empty waiting room for nothing," she said. "But there, separated from life's distractions, in my despair, I became aware that I was not alone, another was there waiting for me. I was in God's waiting room! I marveled that the seemingly illogical route that took me there had stripped me of all the extras so I could come face to face with the reality of relationship with God."

"As for God, His way is perfect." To those of us who are in pain or tired, frustrated, panicky, or angry about waiting, the words of 2 Samuel 1–8 bring hope and instruction.

Waiting on God is never a waste of time. Though David had to wait to become king of Israel, the Scriptures and history show us the amazing effect this delay had on David and the nation. As David was learning to wait on God during his fugitive years, the loosely connected tribes of Israel under Saul were beginning to see their need to unify. But even after King Saul's death it still took seven and a half more years and a tragic civil war before all Israel was convinced unification was essential.

Finally the whole of Israel saw David as the strong leader who could guide the nation out of its chaotic mess. Israel was now ready to become one nation. All the tribes sent large representations to David, begging him to become their king. David wisely took advantage of their enthusiasm and secured commitments from the people.

During Saul's increasingly lax rule, David had observed the need for unity among the greatly disunited tribes. Now David is in the enviable position of saying, in effect, "If you want me as king, here are the conditions." David's wait intensified among the people an awareness of their need to unify and their willingness to do so. Though we do not know the specifics of the covenant that David and the people signed (2 Samuel 5:3), we can infer from what took place later that the covenant must have included guarantees to secure a unified central government, organization, and taxation. God's way had not been slow; it had been effective.

While the elders of Israel and David were signing a covenant in Hebron, a demonstration of unity and enthusiasm took place throughout the country. Thousands of eager men from every tribe marched toward Hebron to declare David their king. Israel had never before known anything like this. Statistics in 1 Chronicles 12:24–37 account for approximately 339,600 warriors and 1,222 chiefs marching to Hebron. National unity and spiritual optimism proceeded through a country torn by civil war. This acclaim is even more amazing when one pictures the scene of hundreds of thousands of men shouting allegiance to a man who had been a fugitive. Now, as one body, the nation lines up behind David. Without resorting to hatred, revenge, scheming, or plotting, David is recognized as king by all Israel. Through God's sovereign working, David now becomes the unifier of the nation. God's faithfulness to David is evident.

David's respect for God and his ways was so different from that of King Saul. Saul ignored the ark, which was seemingly forgotten in Abinadab's home. David made the transporting of the ark to Jerusalem, as well as building a special place for it, one of his first priorities as king. When the ark was placed in the nation's political capital, godly worship was restored to the whole country. Whereas King Saul at one time murdered most of the priesthood, David humbly revered and respected the priests.

Cultural Insights

Jerusalem, the New Capital: David chose Jerusalem as the capital of a united Israel because of its strategic location. Jerusalem had been a neutral site, known as the city of Jebus until its capture by David. Its location, therefore, did not show favor to either side but was one all sides could agree on. The site was also strategic militarily since it was naturally protected by valleys on all sides except the north.

Jerusalem became the political capital of Israel when the army of men David had so carefully organized and trained during his time in exile, turned to support him. When David brought the ark of the covenant to Jerusalem to be housed in a tabernacle, he restored proper worship on a national scale. Jerusalem thus became the religious as well as the political center for all of Israel (see 2 Samuel 6–7).

After David captured the Jebusite fortress, he took up residence there and renamed it the "City of David," and Jerusalem "entered upon its historic career which has made it the most sacred and wonderful city of the world; a city, moreover, with a future even more wonderful than all its glorious and tragic past."[1]

Study Lesson 3

Daily Discovery I   **David, King of Israel**

1. a.   What did all the tribes of Israel finally realize about David (2 Samuel 5:1–3)?

    b.   What does the people's declaration (2 Samuel 5:1–2) teach us about God (see also 1 Samuel 16:1–13)?

    c.   How does this event encourage you? Be specific.

2. a.   If David was about fifteen years old when the events of 1 Samuel 16 took place, how long did he have to wait to experience God's promise (2 Samuel 5:4–5)?

    b.   What does this reveal about David?

With Him in Life's Struggles

c. Has there been a time in your life yet when you have waited to experience a particular promise from God? Can you explain the promise, your reactions to it, and the result of this?

Daily Discovery II **Jerusalem becomes a governmental center (2 Samuel 5:6-16)**

3. a. When the Jebusites said that the "lame and the blind could turn David away" from the city, they meant that their Jebusite city was invincible. Did David listen to the taunts of the enemy? What did he do? What does this indicate about David and about God (2 Samuel 5:6–9)?

b. Write a brief outline of a situation in your life that you perceive to be impossible. Now state two things you have learned about God so far in 2 Samuel.

c. What new insights do you have into your "impossibility"?

4. a. According to 1 Chronicles 11:4–25 and 12:8–18, what type of men did the Lord gather around David to help him lead the nation? (List at least three characteristics.)

b.   Why were men with these characteristics especially helpful to David at this point in his life?

c.   What were the men like who came to David in the beginning (1 Samuel 22:1–2)? What may David have learned as he tried to lead this group? Why might this have been good preparation for leading a war-torn nation?

5.   What was David's secret to success? What can you learn from this (2 Samuel 5:10)?

6.   Because of David's numerous leadership responsibilities, he didn't have time to develop "house-plans" for his home. In light of this, what great encouragement comes in 2 Samuel 5:11–12, and how does David interpret the event? What does such an interpretation reveal about David?

Daily Discovery III   **David's early days as king of Israel**

7.   a.   How did David handle his first real crisis as king (2 Samuel 5:17–20)? What guidelines do you see here that can help you as you face difficulties this week?

With Him in Life's Struggles

b.   If you have the opportunity, share one or more of these guidelines with a friend or family member this week and record the results. Be prepared to share these in your groups.

8.   Summarize David's view of God's part in the Philistine battle (2 Samuel 5:20)?

9.   a.   What did David do when the same problem arose again?

b.   What qualities do you observe in David during his first two tests as king?

c.   What do you learn about God from these events?

d.   What personal significance does studying these experiences of King David have on your life?

Daily Discovery IV   **Jerusalem becomes Israel's religious center (2 Samuel 6)**

As king, David tried to restore the ark of God to a place of prominence so that once again worship of the Lord could become the nation's central focus. David wanted to give the nation a religious center as well as a governmental one.

10. a.   Read 2 Samuel 6:1–7. Specific instructions about how to transport the ark had been

given to Israel hundreds of years before in Numbers 4:4–15. As you compare these instructions with the account in 2 Samuel 6:1–7, what do you discover?

b. What appears to be the attitude of those bringing the ark to Jerusalem? What does this say about David and the people of Israel? (Consider David's reactions to what took place at the threshing floor of Nacon. Why do you think David reacted as he did?)

Daily Discovery V **David and the nation learn an important lesson**

11. Through the seemingly confusing and unfair events of 2 Samuel 6:1–7, what was David forced to search out, consider, and learn (see 1 Chronicles 15:1–2, 11–16, 25–28, along with 2 Samuel 6:11–15)?

12. a. As you consider 2 Samuel 6:7 and 1 Chronicles 15:11–13, what crucial concept do you think God wanted His people to understand? What personal challenge is this to you?

b. Can you think of a time you tried to do something for God but not in His way? What happened? What happened when God's work was done in God's way (see 1 Chronicles 15 and 16)?

13. a. In contrast to David, what was the attitude of his wife Michal (2 Samuel 6:16)?

Compare her reaction and the praise celebration of 2 Samuel 6:12–22. What may have been the basis for her attitude?

b. Michal's attitude results in action. What kind of a reception did she give David when he arrived home after a day of great joy? Why? Describe David's response.

c. Personalize God's message to you in this section.

Key Principles from Lesson 3

1. God is faithful; He will do what He says (2 Samuel 5:1–5).

2. When God calls us to a task, He is faithful to perform the impossible (2 Samuel 5:6–12).

3. Knowing that the Lord God Almighty is with us is the basis for true greatness (2 Samuel 5:10).

4. In a time of crisis, take time to go to the Lord (2 Samuel 5:17–25).

5. Take time to get instructions from the Lord and then follow them (2 Samuel 5:17–25).

6. Revere the Lord (2 Samuel 6:1–12).

7. When God gives us ways to reverence Him, we should be faithful to obey them (2 Samuel 6).

Lesson 4

God's Plan Is Great

Memory Verse: "How great you are, O Sovereign LORD! There is no one like you, and there is no God but you, as we have heard with our own ears" (2 Samuel 7:22).

> How can I give thanks for the things you have
> done for me?
> Things so undeserved yet you gave to prove
> your love for me.
> The voices of a million angels could not
> express my gratitude,
> All that I am and ever hope to be, I owe it all to
> Thee.
> To God be the glory . . . for the things He has
> done.
> *—Andraé Crouch,* "My Tribute"

Have you ever felt like this—overwhelmed by God's unfolding plan for you? This song could summarize David's heart response to God's plan for him, revealed through the prophet Nathan. David, however, had not always been filled with wonder and awe for God's plan. During the difficult days recorded in 1 Samuel 27:1, David appeared to have lost hope. He thought, "One of these days I will be destroyed by the hand of Saul. The best thing I can do is to escape to the land of the Philistines."

What a contrast in 2 Samuel 7 to see the place to which God has brought David. David is now king over the country from which he had been forced to flee and has led Israel in subduing the enemy nations around her. In chapter 7, God reveals an amazing plan to David. This strategic message was most likely given to David at the height of his reign, when the successful wars listed in 2 Samuel 8 and 10 had made Israel the major nation in the Fertile Crescent and had made King David world-famous. (Note: the chronological sequence of 2 Samuel 6–10 was probably broken so that chapter 6 could tell the complete history of the religious movement under David.)

God's plan may have seemed unbelievable to David at first. But as God spoke through Nathan the prophet David began to understand that the events of his life would not only affect history but also stretch victoriously into eternity.

With humility and awe, David responded to God, "Who am I, O Sovereign LORD, and what is my family, that you have brought me this far? . . . How great you are, O Sovereign LORD! . . . Your words are trustworthy, and you have promised these good things to your servant" (2 Samuel 7:18, 22, 28).

It is possible that today you and I may not feel that God's sovereign plan for us is wonderful. We may be able to identify more with David's desert experiences (see 1 Samuel 19–30) than with his successes. Yet 2 Samuel 7 should bring us hope, for God's sovereign plan for David did not end in hopelessness in the desert but in a victory David will enjoy forever.

Study Lesson 4

Daily Discovery I   **David's great desire**

1. a. What comparison did David make between his own house and God's, and what does this indicate about David (2 Samuel 7:1–2)?

b. David didn't just feel bad about this observation, he desired to do something about it. What did David intend to do, and why (2 Samuel 7:1–2; 1 Kings 8:17–18)?

c. David sought to do something about his observations. Think of one specific thing you can do about a desire you have in your heart.

2. a. When David shared his observations and conclusions with Nathan, what was the prophet's first response (2 Samuel 7:3)? According to 1 Kings 8:18–19, what thoughts did God have concerning the desire of David's heart?

b. In light of what follows in 2 Samuel 7:4–13, what do you conclude about Nathan's first reaction (see also Isaiah 55:8–9)? What practical lesson do you draw from this situation, and how can you apply it to your life?

3. In God's message to David through the prophet Nathan in 2 Samuel 7:4–16, who was going to build a "house"? What type of house was God talking about (state the verse references that support your answer)?

Daily Discovery II **God's covenant with David**

With Him in Life's Struggles

4. a. Why was David denied the privilege of building the temple for God? Why was his son Solomon given the honor of building the temple (1 Chronicles 22:6–10; 28:2–6; 1 Kings 5:3–5)?

b. Describe a time when you were kept from doing something you thought was good to do.

5. a. A covenant is a legal, binding agreement between two parties. In 2 Samuel 7:11–16, God makes a covenant with David. Using 2 Samuel 7:8–16 as your source, make a list of what God had already done for David. Then list what God states He **will** do for David.

b. Why do you think God took the time to remind David of what He had done in the past? (It may be helpful to think why you also need reminders of what God has done for you.)

c. Putting yourself in David's place, why might these promises have been overwhelming to comprehend?

6. Years after the great promise of 2 Samuel 7:12–16 was given to David, many aspects of the promise were fulfilled. What promises made to David in 2 Samuel 7:12–16 were fulfilled in 1 Kings 8:2–21? What does this suggest to you about the rest of the promise?

Daily Discovery III   **The close relationship between Israel's king and her God**

7.   How long is David's house, throne, and kingdom to continue (2 Samuel 7:16)?

8.   What type of relationship is going to exist between Israel's king and God (2 Samuel 7:14)?

9.   a.   According to Psalm 89:30–32, what responsibilities do David and his descendants have?

b.   What does God promise He will do if David's descendants sin in their role as ruler? What does God state He will not do (2 Samuel 7:14–16; Psalm 89:30–37)?

Daily Discovery IV   **The eternal king of Israel**

Part of the coronation process of Israel's king was the anointing of the king by God's prophet. This anointing was important, for it demonstrated that the person who was designated in this way was God's choice and thus a true king of Israel. In Hebrew the word **Messiah** means "anointed one." In Greek the same concept is found in the word **Christ.** Both terms are kingly words. The **eternal** king of Israel that was to come is referred to as **the** Messiah, or **the** Christ, both meaning **the** anointed one.

48

10. a. In light of the above, when the term **Messiah** or **Christ** is used with the name of Jesus, what does it mean?

b. How is Jesus seen as the king of Israel, the Messiah, the Christ in the following passages?
Matthew 2:1–6
Mark 14:60–65
John 11:23–27
John 12:12–16
John 19:14–22

11. In 2 Samuel 7:12–13 we learn that the eternal king of Israel will be a descendant (or son) of David. Jesus Christ's ancestral lines descend from David through Joseph (see Matthew 1:1–16) and Mary (see Luke 3:23–32). In 2 Samuel 7:14, we discover a father-son relationship between each king of Israel and God.

a. In Hebrews 1:1–8, to whom are the words of 2 Samuel 7:14 specifically applied?

b. How was this close relationship demonstrated in Jesus' life in the following verses?
Luke 3:21–22
Matthew 16:13–17
Matthew 17:1–5
John 10:24–30, 36
John 12:49–50
John 17:1–3

c.   In light of the above, what was the ongoing relationship between God and Israel's kings intended to illustrate?

12. How has your understanding of Jesus as the Messiah, the Christ, grown as you studied these questions? In light of Isaiah 9:6 and 7, Zechariah 9:9, Matthew 1:1 and Mark 11:7–10, how does Jesus relate to the agreement God made with David? What difference can this new understanding make in your life?

13. The preaching of Jesus about the kingdom demanded a response from men. What was the response according to Mark 1:15? What was to be their foremost concern in life (Matthew 6:33)?

Daily Discovery V   **David responds to God**

14. David's response to God's message is found in 2 Samuel 7:18–29. What does this response reveal about David? What clue does this give concerning the person "after God's heart"? Be sure to support your answer with verse references.

15. Though David was not allowed to carry out his great plan, according to 1 Chronicles 22:1–5, what was he able to do? What does this say about his character? What personal application can you make?

16. Name two things you learn about God from 2 Samuel 7. In what way do these characteristics personally encourage you?

Key Principles from Lesson 4

1. The things of God are top priority to the person who is "after God's heart."

2. Our first impression of what sounds right or looks good may not be in agreement with God's will (2 Samuel 7:3–4, 12–13).

3. We must test our plans with God's revealed Word, not by our feelings (2 Samuel 7:4–13).

4. God always has a reason for what He allows in our lives. God's ways are not our ways (1 Kings 5:3–4; Isaiah 55: 8, 9, 11).

5. God's plans for us today touch tomorrow (2 Samuel 7:8–16).

6. We glorify God by how we respond to His will for our lives. We glorify Him when we:
    a. focus on His character and respond in praise
    b. accept His will
    c. humbly submit to His will
    d. thank Him for His ways
    e. trust in His blessing (2 Samuel 7:18–29).

Lesson 5

The Alternative to Hopelessness

Memory Verse: "Give us aid against the enemy, for the help of man is worthless. With God we will gain the victory . . ." (Psalm 60:11 and 12).

"The LORD gave David victory wherever he went" (2 Samuel 8:6, 14). We tend to picture David moving through one victory after another in glorious succession with hardly a stubbed toe! Our lives, though, don't consist of a long line of successes. We experience times of real failure; failure to reach goals, failure as wives, failure as mothers, failure as friends, and saddest of all, failure as God's friends.

The expansion of David's kingdom into a vast empire stretching from the River of Egypt[2] to the Euphrates River is only briefly recorded in the Bible. It is therefore all too easy not to realize how much time in each battle was devoted to hard work, inner struggle, inquiry, and waiting on the Lord.

In this lesson we look behind the scenes of 2 Samuel 8 and study a Psalm David wrote during this period of conquest. We discover that even during a time of victory, David also experienced some periods of failure and hopelessness. In Psalm 60 we read of a situation that would have caused David to despair had he not resolved to hope in the Lord his God.

Challenged by the truths found in this lesson, we discover an alternative to hopelessness. We can choose to hope in God.

Cultural Insights

David's strong leadership: At the same time that 2 Samuel 8 outlines Israel's triumphs over her adversaries, it also indicates what had happened at home. Israel, under David's wise, God-inspired leadership, was finally unified. The jealousy, resentment, hatred, and bitterness that characterized the interaction between the tribes, making them easy prey for their enemies, was set aside for a great goal—national unity. The separate tribes saw national unity as vital if they were ever to accomplish what God had planned for them as a nation. Foreign wars against adversaries cannot be fought without a strong home base. And now Israel had a strong home base.

The national unity and strong home base achieved under David's rule points to his strong leadership. Although the tribes evidently didn't appreciate it very much in the beginning, David forced the people to discover the joys of unity. This new awareness was actually made possible through the policies and stipulations David negotiated with the people *before* he accepted kingship (see 2 Samuel 5:3). These policies were designed to guarantee true central government, and the tribes were forced to follow them if they wanted David as their king. Now, as Israel confronts its enemies, the tribes are able to stand together as one nation.

David's time as a fugitive, as well as his residence with the economically superior Philistines, prepared him for military leadership. He had firsthand acquaintance with the formulas and methods the Philistines used in the production of arms.

David's Army: The core of the army was most likely made up of the original 600 men from David's fugitive days. To this group was added a standing army of 288,000 trained men. This army operated on a monthly rotating system that involved 24,000 of them each month. However, all were ready for immediate action should the need arise. Finally, David provided for a group of foreign mercenaries composed of Cherithites and Pelethrites who formed a private bodyguard for the king.

It appears that David did not intentionally seek to go to war, but he simply took a stand when the need arose and tried to win. And David continually did win. Thus, Israel's borders expanded until all the land that was promised to Abraham's seed centuries before (Genesis 15:18) was under David's authority. Following the conquests, David's rule extended from the River of Egypt in the south to the Euphrates River in the north. In his day, David was probably the strongest ruler in the world.

Study Lesson 5

Daily Discovery I **David's triumphs**

1. Read 2 Samuel 8. Second Samuel 8 is of great historic value for it records Israel's emergence at the beginning of the 10th century B.C. as the leading nation in the Fertile Crescent.

2. Turn to the back of your Bible to a map of the Empire of David. Follow the conquests of David, referring to 2 Samuel 8. Which of these adversaries (the land areas are mostly under new names today) are currently a problem to Israel?

3. a. David ruled from the River of Egypt to the Euphrates in the north. To whom did God promise this land area centuries before (Genesis 15:18–21)?

b.   Reflecting on Genesis 15:18–21 and 2 Samuel 8, what do you learn about God that can affect your attitude to your circumstances?

4.   What reason does Scripture give for David's ability to accomplish great conquests (2 Samuel 8:6, 14)? What does this suggest to you personally?

5.   What characteristics of David's rule helped unify the fragmented tribes of Israel (2 Samuel 8:15; see "Cultural Insights" above)? In what area of your life today can that same key be applied? State at least one specific way.

6.   What did David consistently do with the treasures that came from the conquests (2 Samuel 8:6–12)?

Daily Discovery II   **David's thoughtful kindness**

7.   Read 2 Samuel 9. At the height of David's power, when all the enemies of Israel had been defeated, what did David take time to do (2 Samuel 9:1–5)? Why (1 Samuel 20:12–17, 42)?

8. a. Why may Mephibosheth have experienced fear when he came before David (2 Samuel 9:6–7)?

b. What did David do for Mephibosheth (2 Samuel 9:7–13)? What was the basis of this kindness (2 Samuel 9:1)?

9. a. What qualities do David's actions reveal in 2 Samuel 9? Why are these actions characteristic of one who loves God?

b. Stop and ask the Lord to help you remember any important promise you have made to your husband, child, or friend that has not been kept. Ask the Lord to empower you to keep your promise in the best way. Be prepared to share with your group any action taken.

Daily Discovery III **The great danger**

In 2 Samuel 10 we get a closer look at one of David's conquests. It appears that the battle mentioned in 2 Samuel 8:3–6 was a major incident that occurred during the course of a great war against the Ammonites and their allies (2 Samuel 10–11). This great war was the major danger to David's kingdom.

10. Read 2 Samuel 10. What kindness is shown by David in chapter 10, and to whom is it given? What is the response to the kindness? What was the result?

11. a. At the beginning of the battle recorded in 2 Samuel 10:6–12, what one word would have described the circumstances Israel faced?

b. When Joab saw that the battle with the Ammonites and their allies was not going well, what did he do? Summarize 2 Samuel 10:9–15 in your own words.

c. In spite of how things had looked at the beginning, what happened (2 Samuel 10:13–19)?

d. What principle from this passage can you apply to your life?

Daily Discovery IV and V   **David determines to trust God**

12. Read Psalm 60.

The great war with the Ammonites was the major threat to David's kingdom. As leader of the nation, David wisely brought his awareness of the danger before the Lord. Though we often talk about our problems, we don't always bring our difficulties and fears to the Lord in prayer as David did. Through the Psalms, we are allowed to see inside David as he faces the awesome task of battling a powerful enemy. From this man whose heart was after God we can learn principles that will help us cope with difficulties.

13. Why did David want to see his "house" remain forever? How is his reason different from that of many rulers today (2 Samuel 7:25–26)?

14. In contrast to the brief account in 2 Samuel 10, Psalm 60 gives the impression that this period of conquest was not easy for David. If it were not for Psalm 60, "we should have no inkling of the resilience of David's hostile neighbors at the peak of his power. His very success brought its dangers of alliances among his enemies (see 2 Samuel 8:5), and of battles far from home. At such a moment, when his main force was with him near the Euphrates (2 Samuel 8:3), Edom evidently took her chance to fall upon Judah from the south. The setting of the Psalm, then, is the deflating news of havoc at home (vv. 1–3), and of a defeat, apparently, at the first attempt to avenge it (v. 10)."[3]

As you read through Psalm 60, make a list of some of the circumstances and feelings that David and his people experienced.

15. a. Psalm 60:3 makes clear that the outward crisis was matched by inward confusion and shock. Describe a time when your circumstances did not appear to line up with what you knew was true about God.

b. David makes sense out of this chaotic time by tracing the hard things right back to God (Psalm 60:1–3) and seeing the entire situation under God's ultimate control. Name a situation in which you need to do the same.

16. a. Using your own words, summarize the prayer of faith found in Psalm 60:5 and 11, listing David's bold requests to God.

b. In brief, what is God's strong response to this prayer in Psalm 60:6–8. How does this personally encourage you?

17. a. David humbly sees that the situation is beyond his own resources. According to Psalm 60:9–12, what is David now keenly aware of?

b. Although he is in the midst of adverse circumstances, where does David place his hope (Psalm 60:12)?

c. Stop and claim this same hope over your difficulties, even if all the statements don't specifically apply to your present circumstances.

Key Principles from Lesson 5

1. We do not need to use human ways to be successful. We need the help of God Almighty (2 Samuel 8:6, 14)!

2. Administration of a nation, a church, or a home with justice and righteousness promotes unity (2 Samuel 8:15).

3. A wise leader remembers to be kind. We are never too important to express thoughtful kindness (2 Samuel 9).

4. In spite of how bad circumstances look, God is always in control and will bring about His perfect plan (2 Samuel 10).
5. Therefore, when the circumstances are set against us, we cannot lose when we follow the Lord and His ways (2 Samuel 10:19).

6. We never waste time when we bring difficulties and fears of danger before the Lord (Psalm 60).

7. Apart from God, the help of other people is worthless (Psalm 60:11). With God, we will gain the victory (Psalm 60:12).

8. Our purpose in whatever we do is to glorify God's name (2 Samuel 7:26).

Lesson 6

The Turning Point

Memory Verse: "Then I acknowledged my sin to you and did not cover up my iniquity. I said, 'I will confess my transgressions to the LORD'—and you forgave the guilt of my sin" (Psalm 32:5).

The phone rang. The tragic story was relayed. The two had ministered together as husband and wife. Now he was gone. She did not cry on the phone. She was in a state of disbelief and shock. There was another woman, and he had moved in with her. The devastating consequences of his decision on their marriage and the lives of their children is still being lived out before us. In over half of the cases currently brought to marriage counselors, adultery is already part of the problem. This problem is increasing throughout our society. In today's culture, adultery is casually accepted by many and even promoted by some.

Because of this we have much to learn from 2 Samuel 11, painful as it is to read. The passage relates one of the most tragic stories in all of Scripture because years of a godly life are severely damaged by one incident of illicit pleasure. The incident of David and Bathsheba is put in the Scripture to give us a warning. It is to show us something of the destructiveness of a willful act of rebellion against God. You see in this passage the damage caused by sin, particularly the sin of adultery. We see also that sin always affects others.

Chapter 11 sadly marks the pivotal point in our study of 2 Samuel. The chapters leading up to 2 Samuel 11 set forth David's victories, but the chapters that follow it emphasize King David's troubles. As chapter 11 begins,

King David is a powerful and important king. Israel's enemies have been conquered, one by one, as David experienced an unbroken series of military successes. In 2 Samuel 11 we see the Israelites take their final stand against their last enemy—the Ammonites. The military expedition against the Ammonite capital of Rabbah was so important that the Israelite army took the ark of God with them into battle. It appears, however, that David did not feel it was important for him to lead his army into this battle. He sent Joab in his place. This decision to compromise was significant for it led to the dramatic turning point in David's career.

David came close to the heart of God and through the Psalms declared with great affection what God is like. But at this point in his life, David tramples underfoot the intimacy he had known, and he sins against the Lord. When we see him fall, we unconsciously cry out, "Oh no, David, not you!" How hard it is to watch this hero fail.

Why did David fall into this sin? Certainly the culture itself encouraged the sin. Kings in David's time had the right to do and have anything they wanted. Did David begin to think like his culture? Did the fact that David was so successful influence his thinking? Success can bring its own brand of temptation. Psychologists today point out that a sense of power grows in the mind of those who are successful. Often accompanying this is the mistaken idea that whatever they do is right. Dr. Harry Johnson in his book *Executive Lifestyles*[4] publishes the results of his study of a large number of executives. After interviewing 6000 business executives, Dr. Johnson stated that 20 percent engaged in extra-marital affairs. But he also discovered that as the level of success and financial remuneration went up, so did this percentage.

As you study the biblical text in this lesson, other factors that led to David's fall will surface. However, there came the moment when David made a decision to yield to the temptation of adultery.

In studying this lesson Saint Augustine's words are poignant for us: "David's fall should put upon their guard all who have not fallen, and save from despair all those who have fallen."

Study Lesson 6

Daily Discovery I   **David's sin**

1.   Read 2 Samuel 11.

2.   What does 2 Samuel 11:1 imply about the character of David's leadership at this time? What mistake opened the door to temptation?

3.   a.   Sin is often the result of a process. Show how the sin process discussed in James 1:14–15 is illustrated by 2 Samuel 11:2–5. What had David already given into that may have provided a stepping stone to the sin of 2 Samuel 11 (see 2 Samuel 5:13 along with Deuteronomy 17:15–18)?

b.   How have you been made aware of the sin process, described in James 1:14–15, in your own life?

c.   Becoming aware of our seemingly innocent first steps toward sin can keep us from falling again. Have you ever asked God to reveal to you where you first went wrong (or consistently go wrong) in a certain area? If not, do so now. If so, what did He make you aware of?

4. a. Having committed the initial sin, what did David feel compelled to do next (2 Samuel 11:6–8)?

   b. Contrast David and Uriah at this time.

   c. Why do you think David was so irritated with Uriah's responses?

5. a. Proceeding rapidly in his tragic decline, David's previous sins lead him to drastic action. What sin is he now guilty of and why do you think he felt the need to do this (2 Samuel 11:14–17, 25)? How can the chosen and victorious David have reached a point so low?

   b. From a human point of view, does it look as if David is "getting away" with his sin (2 Samuel 11:26–27)? Explain. What was God aware of as He saw David's actions (2 Samuel 11:27)? How is this a warning to you?

6. a. What two principles can you develop from 2 Samuel 11?

   b. How might you apply these principles to your life? Be specific.

Daily Discovery II   **David's inner struggles over his sin**

In the time lapse between David's sin and his confession, what went on inside him? Once again the Psalms give insight into David's inner struggles. Through his psalms David's heart is laid bare and we wonder if ours could be so sincere.

7.   Carefully observe the passage, making a list of physical and mental or emotional problems experienced by David after he sinned (see Psalms 32:3–4 and 38).

Physical Problems / Mental or Emotional Problems

8.   What key does David give in Psalm 32:3 that reveals why miseries have come upon him? What does this suggest to you personally?

Daily Discovery III   **Nathan's rebuke**

9.   What did God do about David's sin and his resulting misery (2 Samuel 12:1)?

10. a.   How did Nathan get David to recognize his sin (2 Samuel 12:1–4)? Why do you think this approach was wise? In what situations might you use Nathan's approach?

b.   What point did God make to David in 2 Samuel 12:7–9? How should you apply this principle to your own life when you desire things that are contrary to God's Word?

11. In light of his recent actions, what was David despising (2 Samuel 12:9)? What does this suggest to you about your actions?

12. a.   Though there is forgiveness, nevertheless there are consequences of sin. What did God say the consequences of David's sin would be (2 Samuel 12:10–12, 14)?

b.   Think of a modern example of a sin that makes "the enemies of the Lord show utter contempt" (2 Samuel 12:14).

Daily Discovery IV   **David's confession**

13. a.   In terms of our culture today, David's response to Nathan's confrontation is significant. How (2 Samuel 12:13)? Is his response surprising to you? Why?

b.   How is David's confession and God's response, through Nathan, an example of the New Testament truth stated in 1 John 1:9?

c. What personal application from this chapter can you make?

14. Psalm 51 records David's thoughts after Nathan the prophet came to him. God made a merciful declaration to David through Nathan in 2 Samuel 12:13. According to the Old Testament law of Leviticus 20:10, what could have happened to David at this point?

15. a. What specific action concerning his problem did David take (Psalm 32:3–5)? What did he then encourage others to do (Psalm 32:6)?

b. What will be the results in your life if you respond to sin as David did in Psalm 32:5? (Make your list from Psalm 32:1–2, 5–8, 10–11.)

16. a. Describe the gift (or sacrifice) David desired to give to God as thanksgiving for what He had done for him (Psalm 51:14–17).

b. What changes would there be in your life if you had the attitude David expressed in Psalm 51?

17. State the promise and warning God gives David in Psalm 32:8–9? Why was this good for David to know at this time?

18. a.   In what ways did David speak from experience in his two-part statement found in Psalm 32:10?

   b.   What can you do when Psalm 32:1–10 is your experience (see also Psalm 32:11)?

19. a.   What is significant about David's response to his son's illness and consequent death (2 Samuel 12:14–23)?

   b.   After he confessed to the Lord, how was David able to be sensitive to Bathsheba during her time of difficulty? How did God encourage Bathsheba (2 Samuel 12:24–25)?

   c.   The name Solomon means peace. Why was this a significant name for David to choose for his son?

20. State ways God's blessing is restored to David (2 Samuel 12:24–30).

Key Principles from Lesson 6

1.   Irresponsibility to a task God has given us may make us vulnerable to temptation (2 Samuel 11:1).

2.   Compromising with Scripture weaves a thread that entraps (2 Samuel 3:2–5; 5:13–16).

3. Dwelling on lustful thoughts leads to sin (2 Samuel 11:2–5).

4. One sin leads to another unless repentance breaks the cycle (2 Samuel 11).

5. We never get away with sin (2 Samuel 11:27; 12:1).

6. Not dealing with our sin literally destroys us on the inside (Psalm 32:3).

7. When we sin, we sin against God (2 Samuel 12:9).

8. The person who is after God's heart does not rationalize sin but is straightforward: "I have sinned" (2 Samuel 12:13).

9. True repentance results in peace with God (1 John 1:9; 2 Samuel 12:13).

10. Sin has long-range consequences, even though God forgives and our relationship with Him is restored (2 Samuel 12:10–12, 14).

11. When we have peace with God, we are sensitive to the needs of others (2 Samuel 12:24–25).

12. When we have peace with God, we have joy in the Lord. Happy is the person who knows he or she is forgiven (Psalm 32:1, 11).

13. A broken and contrite heart is a holy gift to God (Psalm 51:14–17).

14. Unfailing love surrounds the person who trusts in the Lord (Psalm 32:10).

Lesson 6: The Turning Point

Lesson 7

Consequences—
The Chain Reaction

Memory Verse: "Create in me a pure heart, O God, and renew a steadfast spirit within me" (Psalm 51:10).

The Ringstrasse that encircles the city of Vienna is a busy street, but especially so during evening rush hour. Impatient drivers are tempted to take chances to speed up their progress. That's what happened to me recently. The traffic was terrible! Suddenly I saw a car cut unexpectedly into the lane of the red car in front of me. The driver of the red car put on his brakes to avoid an accident, so I had to as well. With relief, I was able to stop inches from the red car. But as I did so, I saw in the rear view mirror the anxious look of the driver behind me who amazingly was able to stop just short of my fender. Again I relaxed. But then the sound of a crash split the air. The car behind me was hit from the rear as a fourth car tried to brake. His unsuccessful attempt thrust the car behind me into my car forcing me into the car ahead. What a chain reaction! Four cars were in an accident as a result of one selfish, impatient driver.

The chain reaction of sin is like that pile up of cars. Sin is not a private matter that touches just the individual. It always affects someone else.

The effect of David's sin on his family and his kingdom demonstrates this fact. With a broken and contrite heart, David had confessed his sin and experienced God's forgiveness. Thus David could declare: "Blessed is he whose transgressions are forgiven, whose sins are covered . . . I acknowledged my sin to you . . . and you forgave the guilt of my sin" (Psalm 32:1, 5). David could then pray in faith: "Create in me a pure heart, O God, and renew a steadfast spirit within me" (Psalm 51:10). However, while genuine repentance does restore the joy of relationship with God, sin still has its consequences, and sometimes those consequences are permanent.

God had forgiven David's adultery and murder, but there had been a baby and now the baby was dead and David's faithful follower and supporter was dead. Then during the twentieth year of David's reign, a chain reaction of consequences became visible as the selfishness of David's oldest son, Amnon, ushered in a long series of family and public troubles.

During all of these troubles, God never left David. When David called out to the Lord in humility, he experienced the comfort, guidance, and power of God.

In many ways this week's lesson may be hard, not because the lesson is difficult to understand, but because it is so sad. Though the events of 2 Samuel 13 and 14 took place more than three thousand years ago, it is as relevant to our day as the morning newspaper. As we approach these two chapters, 2 Timothy 3:16–17 is a challenge to us: "All Scripture is God-breathed, and is useful for teaching, rebuking, correction and training in righteousness, so that the man of God may be thoroughly equipped for every good work."

Study Lesson 7

Daily Discovery I   **Trouble in David's household**

Absalom and Tamar were David's children by Maacah, the daughter of the king of Geshur (2 Samuel 3:3). Amnon was their step brother in that he was David's son by Ahinoam, the Jezreelitess (2 Samuel 3:2).

1. Read 2 Samuel 13:1–17. David's son Amnon had a problem with temptation. What does 2 Samuel 13:1–2 indicate he was doing about his temptation?

2. a. Read 2 Samuel 13:8–15. Did Amnon get what he wanted? Did it make him happy? Explain.

   b. What was Amnon's attitude toward Tamar (2 Samuel 13:15–17)?

3. a. Do you think Tamar was guilty or innocent in this incident? Why or why not? Support your answer from the passage (2 Samuel 13:8–14).

   b. Summarize in your own words Tamar's response to her situation (2 Samuel 13:18–20).

4. What do you learn from this passage that would help you resist temptations that you face?

Daily Discovery II   **David's response to Amnon's injustice**

5. a. What did David do about his son's immoral act (2 Samuel 13:21)? What might this

indicate about David's parenting style? How do you view David's response in light of God's law revealed to Israel in Leviticus 20:17?

b.   In what way may David's lack of action have influenced Absalom's future behavior seen in 2 Samuel 13:22–29?

6.   What possible weakness does David reveal as he interacts with Absalom in 2 Samuel 13:24–27?

7.   What practical application for your household is found in this lesson?

Daily Discovery III   **Absalom's response**

8.   Trace the progression of Absalom's response to the injustice done to his sister (2 Samuel 13:22–29).

9.   a.   What was Absalom actually doing when he decided to carry out the plan described in 2 Samuel 13:22–29 (Leviticus 19:17–18; Hebrews 10:30)?

b.   What consequences did Absalom bring upon himself as a result of doing things his way and not God's (2 Samuel 13:37–39)? (See also Deuteronomy 32:35 and Hebrews 10:30.)

Daily Discovery IV and V   **David's response to Absalom's sin**

10. Read 2 Samuel 14.

11. How did David handle his son Absalom's sin (2 Samuel 13:37–39; 14:1–14)? What picture do you have here of David?

12. a.   What characterized David's behavior toward his son even after he allowed Absalom to return to Jerusalem (2 Samuel 14:23–29)?

    b.   What was the result of David's way of handling Absalom's sin (2 Samuel 13:28–38, 14:28–33)?

    c.   Does it appear that Absalom ever repented of his sin? Does it appear that David applied the same principle at home that he used to rule the country (see 2 Samuel 8:15)? Explain.

13. How did Absalom view himself? What may have encouraged him to have this view (see 2 Samuel 15:1–6)?

14. List several principles about the relationships seen in 2 Samuel 14. How might you apply one of these principles to your life?

Key Principles from Lesson 7

1. Don't dwell on temptation (2 Samuel 13:2, 4).

2. Counsel must be evaluated in light of the Word of God (2 Samuel 13:5–7).

3. Giving in to temptation will not make us happy (2 Samuel 13:15).

4. When injustice falls under our jurisdiction, we must deal with it. If we are a parent, we must deal with our child's unjust acts (2 Samuel 8:15; 13–21).

5. Unjust people who are not made to see their errors feel justified in their act (2 Samuel 15:1–6).

6. Lack of firmness encourages continued injustice (2 Samuel 13:24–29).

7. Avenging is the Lord's job, not ours (Hebrews 10:30).

8. Forgiveness and acceptance go hand in hand. When we forgive, we accept (2 Samuel 14:21, 24, 32, 33). Restoration is key.

Lesson 8

The Betrayal and the Support

Memory Verse: "My soul clings to you; your right hand upholds me" (Psalm 63:8).

Pain, confusion, unbelief are on her face as she sits opposite me at the kitchen table sharing her heart. "Where did it come from? How did it happen? I can't fit it together. We have been friends for years, in my mind close friends. We walked through many things together. In her difficult days I encouraged her and she in turn helped me. Going to her home was a place of welcome and refreshment for me. And now this! I can't believe she said the words and acted against me as she did. I never guessed what was going on inside her. It's a knife of pain through my heart. I have been betrayed!"

Though the woman sitting across the table is trying to tell me how she feels, I realize no words properly describe the anguish of betrayal. Perhaps you too have known the searing pain of betrayal in a marriage or friendship.

For David, the tragedy of betrayal came from a relationship with a son he loved. Absalom not only wanted to take his father's throne, but he desired to kill him! Here is an example of the tragic result of unresolved conflict. Little sores of bitterness left unchecked in Absalom had festered and spread, causing an irreparable breach. And David despaired. Very likely 2 Samuel 15–18 describes the most difficult time in David's life. In the midst of the disorientation and chaos, he cries out to God, "My soul clings to you; your right hand upholds me" (Psalm 63:8). David's testimony of divine support in the midst of deep anguish is a declaration of hope to us today.

Study Lesson 8

Daily Discovery I **Conspiracy against David**

In this lesson we continue to watch David experience something of the sorrow his disobedience and crime had caused his heavenly Father. David learns this pain through his own children.

1. Read 2 Samuel 15:1–12.

2. Observe and then list Absalom's character traits as seen in 2 Samuel 13:19–29, 32, 37–38 and 2 Samuel 14:21–33.

3. What method did Absalom use to turn the hearts of the people away from David (2 Samuel 15:1–6)? What similar appeals occur today?

4. What disturbs you about Absalom's interaction with his father in 2 Samuel 15:7–10? Why?

5. What important role had Ahithophel played in David's life? How did that role change according to 2 Samuel 15:12, 31? What does this suggest to you?

With Him in Life's Struggles

6. The conspiracy quickly grew to large proportions. What does this indicate (2 Samuel 15:12–13)?

Daily Discovery II **David's flight**

7. In the midst of the shocking and painful news of the conspiracy, David makes a crucial decision. What is David's appraisal of his situation (2 Samuel 15:14)?

8. Put yourself in David's place and consider what the officials' response would have meant to you (see 2 Samuel 15:15). Explain a situation in which you have made (or need to make) a statement similar to that of David's servants.

9. Read and carefully observe the events of 2 Samuel 15:16–16:14, trying to imagine the emotions of such an hour. List your observations of the scene. Example: As David left this city, he was crying, his head was covered, and he didn't have any shoes on his feet (2 Samuel 15:30).

10. Scripture records various reactions to David personally as well his desperate situation. State the reactions of the following people along with David's response to them.

   a.   David's servants (2 Samuel 15:14–15).

b.   Ittai, the Gittite (2 Samuel 15:18–22).

c.   Zadok and Abiathar, the priests (2 Samuel 15:24–29).

d.   Ahithophel (2 Samuel 15:12, 31).

e.   Hushai, the Arkite (2 Samuel 15:32–37).

f.   Ziba (2 Samuel 16:1–4; 19:24–30).

g.   Shimei (2 Samuel 16:5–8, 13).

11. What distinction is made between David's two close counselors, Ahithophel and Hushai (2 Samuel 15:12, 37; 1 Chronicles 27:33)? What does this distinction indicate to you?

12. a.   What does David's response to his humiliating and desperate circumstances tell you about him (2 Samuel 15:13–16:12)?

b.   According to David's own words, what did he have to offer those who stood by him (2 Samuel 15:19–20)?

c.   What attitude does David reveal in his response to Shimei (2 Samuel 16:5–12)?

d.   As you read through David's responses, what truth about God does David constantly acknowledge?

Daily Discovery III   **David's heart revealed**

King David wrote some of the sweetest and most affirmative psalms during this sad time in his life. Here David reveals his heart and as a result is an encouragement to future generations of believers.

13. a.   Read Psalm 3. This psalm reveals some of David's thought processes as he flees from his son, Absalom. How is David able to face the devastating issue before him (Psalm 3:1–4)?

b.   Because of David's confidence in the Lord (Psalm 3:3–4), what is he able to do, according to Psalm 3:5–6?

c.   Knowing his God, what could David say by faith (Psalm 3:7–8)? Put your answer in your own words.

d.   What truth about God encourages you most from this Psalm? How will you apply it to your life? Be specific.

Daily Discovery IV   **David longs for God**

14. Read Psalm 63. David wrote when his circumstances forced him to live in the wilderness of Judah.

15. a.   At this point in his life, when David had seemingly lost everything, what does David state he needs in order to be satisfied (Psalm 63:1)?

b.   What affirmation in Psalm 63:1 indicates why David could respond as he did to his circumstances? In what way do you identify with David here?

16. a.   In Psalm 63, at what point does David mention his problem? Before this point, what would you say was his emphasis?

b.   What insight does this give you about your own prayer life?

c.   According to Psalm 63:8, how is one preserved in the midst of difficulties? In light of this, what should you be doing to be sustained in the difficulties you are presently facing?

d. As you reflect on the circumstances David faced in 2 Samuel 15, how is his reference to himself as king in Psalm 63:9–11 a demonstration of faith?

e. As you think about a difficulty in your life, write a statement that indicates your faith in God.

Daily Discovery V   **Absalom's two counselors**

17. a. Absalom and his followers have triumphantly entered Jerusalem. Briefly summarize the counsel Ahithophel and Hushai give to Absalom (2 Samuel 16:20–17:14).

b. Which counsel did Absalom choose? Why?

c. All seemed lost for David, yet what does 2 Samuel 16:20–17:14 teach about God? Consider how you can apply this to your life and be prepared to share with your group.

18. a. List the ways God ministered to David's need in the midst of his suffering (2 Samuel 17:24–29).

b. Who, in your life, is a similar blessing?

Key Principles from Lesson 8

1.   We serve the Lord by following His Word. We cannot serve the Lord when we break a biblical principle. God's will is consistent with His Word (2 Samuel 15:7–8, 10).

2.   We need to support those who are in leadership (2 Samuel 15:14–37).

3.   True loyalty counts the cost and decides "whether it means life or death, there will your servant be" (2 Samuel 15:21).

4.   Loyalty means being willing to take risks (2 Samuel 15:32–37).

5.   A trustworthy friend is consistent and does not change with the tide (2 Samuel 15:12, 32–34, 37).

6.   In difficult circumstances, the path of wisdom is to realize that God is in control and to accept with a gentle, quiet spirit. One leads to the other (2 Samuel 16:10–12).

7.   We can face difficult issues if we focus on specifics about God. Example: "But you are a shield around me, O LORD; you bestow glory on me and lift up my head" (Psalm 3:3).

8.   God sustains us in difficulties. Therefore, we can sleep peacefully and not be afraid of other people (Psalm 3:5–6).

9.   It is God's job to bring salvation and blessing in our longings (Psalm 3:7–8).

10. Only a growing relationship with God satisfies our longings (Psalm 63:1–5).

11. In times of difficulty, we need to determine that God is our Lord and seek Him earnestly (Psalm 63:1).

12. In prayer, focusing on what God is like helps to put our problem in perspective.

13. Preservation in times of difficulty comes when we cling to God and discover that His right hand upholds us (Psalm 63:8).

14. No matter what the difficulty is, God is always in control and accomplishes His plan (2 Samuel 17:14).

15. God knows what we need and how to meet that need. He knows the perfect way to encourage us (2 Samuel 17:24–29).

Lesson 9

How To Stand When You've Been Flattened

Memory Verse: "On my bed I remember you; I think of you through the watches of the night. Because you are my help, I sing in the shadow of your wings" (Psalm 63:6–7).

Tom, a close friend of ours, was president of a large company for many years. Under his wise and capable leadership, the business had thrived. Then suddenly, unbelievably, at 59 years of age he was fired. The absentee owner of the business was frustrated at our friend's continual refusal to compromise on the financial statistics of the business. This time the owner angrily declared, "That's it. You're out! This organization is mine! I can do what I want with it!" Our friend walked out of his office that day never to return to the responsibility he had known for 15 years.

What do you do when you've been flattened? Like David did in Psalm 3 and Psalm 63, Tom and his wife focused on the character of God and then applied what they knew was true of God to their devastating situation. As a result, they experienced the peace of God even though Tom did not have a job for six months and the prospects of a man of his age getting any work were limited.

Then God Almighty provided for Tom as He had for David 3000 years before when God re-established David as king of Israel. Miraculously Tom was hired to lead another company where he was free to follow biblical business principles. The blessing of God upon Tom and his business now is evident.

There are times in life when we are devastated, broken, and helpless and we don't know what to do next. As David left his beloved Jerusalem, he expressed such feelings to a group of supporters who sought to join him.

"Why should you come along with us? Go back and stay with King Absalom . . . . You came only yesterday. And today shall I make you wander about with us, when I do not know where I am going?" (2 Samuel 15:19–20).

David too was humiliated, weakened, and mocked. Yet in this lesson we see the result of David's decision to look away from the terrible circumstances in his life and to shift his attention to God.

David used even the wakeful hours of the night to remind himself of what his God was like: "On my bed I remember you; I think of you through the watches of the night. Because you are my help, I sing in the shadow of your wings . . ." (Psalm 63:6–7). "But you are a shield around me, O LORD; you bestow glory on me and lift up my head . . . The LORD sustains me. I will not fear the tens of thousands . . ." (Psalm 3:3, 5–6). "Your love is better than life . . ." (Psalm 63:3).

Because of this perspective, David was able to declare by faith, "But the king will rejoice in God; all who swear by God's name will praise Him" (Psalm 63:11).

Cultural Insight

As you read through this lesson, you will find it helpful to note these cultural aspects.

1.   Riding a mule was a sign of royalty. For example, in 1 Kings 1:33 and 38, King David requests that his son, Solomon, ride on his mule. This action indicates Solomon as the successor to the throne. In this week's lesson, we read of Absalom riding into battle on a mule (2 Samuel 18:9).

2.   In the ancient Near East, to "lie with" the king's wives and concubines was tantamount to usurping that king's throne.

Study Lesson 9

Daily Discovery I   **The tragic battle**

1. a.   Read 2 Samuel 18.

    b.   In the midst of the chaos and heartache of the conspiracy, David took time both to focus on God and to get his situation into proper perspective (see Psalms 3 and 63 in Lesson 8). What was one result of this? See 2 Samuel 18:1–2. (The word "mustered" in 2 Samuel 18:1 also means "numbered" and "reviewed.")

    c.   Compare the king's attitudes in 2 Samuel 18:2 and 2 Samuel 11:1. What do you think is the cause of the change in his attitude?

2. a.   What conclusions do David's followers come to in 2 Samuel 18:3? Do you think their reasoning was wise? Why or why not?

    b.   What attitude does David display in his response to the people (2 Samuel 18:4)?

3. a.   What is one of the king's great concerns as his followers depart for battle (2 Samuel 18:5)?

b. What observation do you make as you compare David's concern here with his actions in 2 Samuel 14:24, 28, 30–32? What do you learn from this?

4. a. The sovereign God allowed several factors to help David's small army as it faced the huge but hastily assembled troops under Absalom. Name at least two factors from 2 Samuel 18:6–10.

b. What can you learn about your own impossible situations from this passage?

5. As you consider Joab's words and actions in 2 Samuel 18:10–16 and 19:1–7, what conclusions do you come to about his behavior? Be sure to give the verse references.

6. a. What were the consequences of the attempt to steal the throne from the God-appointed king of Israel (2 Samuel 18:9–17)?

b. Contrast the monument of 2 Samuel 18:17 and that of 2 Samuel 18:18.

Daily Discovery II **The strange victory**

7. What was Ahimaaz's great concern (2 Samuel 18:19–28)?

8. a. What seems to be the priority in the king's mind in 2 Samuel 18:29–33?

b. What does David seem to miss in the news as a result of his sorrow (see 2 Samuel 18:28, 31, 33)? Think of a time when you reacted as David did. Explain.

9. After carefully reading 2 Samuel 19:1–5, list the actions that seem out of character for a victory celebration. What was the reason for this?

10. a. Why would David's grief be so discouraging to his followers?

b. Using your own words, summarize Joab's challenge to David in 2 Samuel 19:5–7.

c. Are there times when we may need to put aside our own sorrows for the good of others? Explain.

Daily Discovery III **David waits at Mahanaim**

11. Summarize the practical dilemma the people of Israel faced in 2 Samuel 19:9–10.

12. What do you see David doing about Israel's dilemma (2 Samuel 19:11–14)?

Daily Discovery IV   **David at the Jordan**

13. Which two men most dreaded the king's return? Why (2 Samuel 15:31; 16:5–13, 21–22)?

14. What does David's interaction with Shimei indicate about the king's attitude of heart (2 Samuel 19:15–23)? Do you think the king handled the situation with Shimei wisely or unwisely?

15. a.   What is revealed when Mephibosheth meets the king (2 Samuel 19:24–30; 16:1–4)?

b.   Describe the king's solution to the problem. Do you think his solution was wise? Why or why not?

16. a.   How did Barzillai support David in his adversity (2 Samuel 17:27–29; 19:31–32)?

b.   What were Barzillai's motives for helping David? Support your answer from Scripture. Think of a person in your life to whom you can be a Barzillai. Explain how you can do this.

17. What was the heart of the argument that took place on King David's return trip to Gilgal (2 Samuel 19:40–43)?

Daily Discovery V **Study observations**

18. a.   Reflect on 2 Samuel 18 and 19. Do you think David submitted to God's discipline (see also 2 Samuel 12:9–12)? Explain.

b.   What did the Lord do for David during his difficulties?

19. In the midst of tragedy, how did David display a heart after God? How did he not?

Key Principles from Lesson 9

1.   We need to focus on God during our difficulties and see our situation from a biblical perspective. We will then be ready to take a stand (Psalm 3; Psalm 63; 2 Samuel 18:1–2).

2.   Because God is sovereign and all-powerful, He can accomplish His purposes with a few people as well as with many (2 Samuel 18:6–10).

3.   Never try to do yourself what God alone can do (2 Samuel 15:10; 18:9–17).

4.   When we are obsessed by a certain thing, we often miss what God has done (2 Samuel 18:28–32).

5.   At times we may need to put aside our own sorrows for the good of others (2 Samuel 19:5–7).

6.   We cannot build a monument to ourselves. God builds the monument (2 Samuel 18:17–18).

7.   When we don't understand God's priorities, we may be tempted to vie for positions of importance (2 Samuel 19:41–43).

With Him in Life's Struggles

Lesson 10

"Oh No, Not a New Problem!"

Memory Verse: He said: "The LORD is my rock, my fortress and my deliverer; my God is my rock, in whom I take refuge, my shield and the horn of my salvation. He is my stronghold, my refuge and my savior—from violent men you save me" (2 Samuel 22:2–3).

The incident made an indelible impression on my mind. Though it took place many years ago, the event is as clear to me as yesterday. It was a Wednesday night. I had slipped into the back pew of our empty church to be quiet and pray. My mind was cluttered. Life was full with small children, my husband's responsibilities in his leadership roles at seminary and church, and the multitudinous needs of others. I wanted to be able to sit alone and think. Struggling to get perspective, I thought, "Coping with one more thing right now would be impossible. It's time for a breather between crises."

I felt sure God knew my need for mental rest and relaxation. It was at that point in my thinking that I became aware for the first time that another person was sitting at the far end of my pew. "Don't look," I thought, "or you'll become involved." However, I turned and faced the young, desperate-looking woman staring at me.

"My name's Myrna," I said. "I feel overwhelmed tonight, but I'm talking to God about it. He is here and will strengthen me."

"My name's Deb. I'm coming off drugs. I need help!"

With those words a difficult and frustrating yet instructive and challenging period in our family's life began.

Today, you may also be saying, "Oh no, not something else, not now!" Perhaps you have just come through a hard time and suddenly you are facing a new storm.

"I just can't handle another difficulty right now!" you exclaim. Most likely David felt the same way as he crossed the Jordan River to be reinstated as the king of Israel after one of the hardest times of his life. Suddenly, David was in the middle of a new crisis that had the potential of doing "more harm than Absalom" (2 Samuel 20:6). "All the men of Israel deserted David to follow Sheba" (2 Samuel 20:2).

The psalms of David written during this difficult period indicate his focus and resulting reliance on the Lord. They give us encouragement and direction when we feel, "This time, I've had it!"

Study Lesson 10

Daily Discovery I   **David faces a new difficulty**

1.   a.   Read 2 Samuel 19:41–43 and 2 Samuel 20:1–7.

b.   What confronted David in the midst of his victorious return to Jerusalem (2 Samuel 19:41–43; 20:1–2)? If you had been in David's position, what emotions would you have experienced?

c.   How does Scripture describe Sheba (2 Samuel 20:1)? What specifically did Sheba do (2 Samuel 20:1–2, 7, 14)?

d. What word or phrase would you use to describe the actions of the men of Israel (2 Samuel 20:2)?

2. a. What did David do about this difficulty (2 Samuel 20:4–6)? What was his priority? Do you think this was wise or unwise? Explain. What might you learn from David's response to Sheba's actions?

b. Why didn't Amasa lead David's troops against Sheba as initially planned (2 Samuel 20:4–6)?

3. How did David "set his house in order" when he returned to Jerusalem (2 Samuel 20:3)?

Daily Discovery II **The encounter**

4. a. Read 2 Samuel 20:8–13.

b. What do Joab's actions toward his cousin Amasa indicate about Joab's character (2 Samuel 20:7–10; see also 2 Samuel 19:11–13)?

c. What was the people's first reaction to Joab's action (2 Samuel 20:11–13)? What happened when the "problem" was removed from sight?

Daily Discovery III   **Destruction is averted**

5.   Read 2 Samuel 20:14–26.

6.   After Sheba arrived at Abel Beth Macaah, what happened to the city (2 Samuel 20:14–15)?

7.   How was the destruction of the city averted (2 Samuel 20:16–22)? As you consider the use of the descriptive word **wise** in this passage, what does it suggest to you?

Note: "Wise words override ruthless policy. At the end not only the woman and the city are saved; something of David's dignity and self-respect are also rescued from Joab's mad, obedient intent."[5]

Daily Discovery IV   **The famine**

With the conclusion of 2 Samuel 20, the last uprising against David ends, and with it the political history of David's reign.

It appears that the five subjects treated in the concluding chapters of 2 Samuel are not a continuation of the book's narrative which ends in 2 Samuel 20. It is impossible, therefore, to know the time of the famine discussed in 2 Samuel 21:1–14.

8.   a.   Read 2 Samuel 21:1–14. When a major difficulty affected those for whom David was responsible, what did he do (2 Samuel 21:1)?

b.   Record a situation in which you need to do as David did.

9.   What reason does God give to David for the hardship that is occurring in his life (2 Samuel 21:1–2)?

10. a.   Compare Israel's judgment with the commitment their forefathers had made years before (Joshua 9:1–27, especially verses 18–21). What does this indicate about God and the commitments His people make?

b.   What did God's people neglect to do before making the original commitment (Joshua 9:14–16)?

c.   In spite of their forefathers' error, were the children of Israel still committed to keeping the promise their forefathers had made (Joshua 9:15–20)? Explain. What was to happen to Israel if they weren't faithful to the commitment (Joshua 9:20)? What took place years later to reinstate this commitment (2 Samuel 21:5–6)?

11. a.   Develop some principles about commitment, using 2 Samuel 21:1–3 and Joshua 9:1–27 as your guide.

b.   In light of the above: 1) as a wife, what specific applications can you make? 2) as a mother, what specific things should be part of your children's training? 3) as a single woman, what specific applications can you make?

Daily Discovery V   **David responds to God's purpose**

12. a.   After David discovers the cause of the famine, what specific actions did he take (2 Samuel 21:2–9)?

b.   State in your own words the priority issue that is at stake (2 Samuel 21:3; Joshua 9:19).

c.   How are David's actions faithful to this priority? To what other commitment is David also being faithful (2 Samuel 21:7; see also 2 Samuel 9:1, 7; 1 Samuel 20:12–17)?

d.   Make a personal application from this passage.

13. In spite of what David had to do as king of Israel, how did he show compassion toward the sorrow of Rizpah (2 Samuel 21:8–14)?

Key Principles from Lesson 10

1. Every difficulty in your life should be entrusted to God (1 Samuel 20).

2. A woman who supports her actions and attitudes with Scripture is wise (2 Samuel 20:16–22).

3. When those we are responsible for are in trouble, we should seek the Lord on their behalf (2 Samuel 21:1).

4. Always seek the Lord before making a serious commitment (Joshua 9:14–16).

5. God expects us to keep our commitments (Joshua 9:16–20).

6. We witness for or against God, depending on how we keep our commitments (Joshua 9:19; 2 Samuel 21:1–2).

7. It is wise to model for our children our faithfulness to commitments.

Lesson 11

Song of Thanksgiving

Memory Verse: "You are my lamp, O LORD; the LORD turns my darkness into light. . . . As for God, his way is perfect; the word of the LORD is flawless. He is a shield for all who take refuge in him" (2 Samuel 22:29, 31; see also Psalm 18:29–30).

We just moved. Sorting, discarding, and treasuring were daily activities. One aspect of this process was particularly enlightening. Almost every day I unearthed quickly jotted prayer requests and written applications of various biblical passages for myself and each of our children. Some of these requests dated as far back as my insecure days as a new mother. To review what God had done through the years in response to prayer enabled me to see His incredible faithfulness.

Knowing now His answers to many of my prayers and seeing the result of His word applied to life, I looked across my desk at pictures of our grown children, and I praised God for the eternal treasure of experiencing Him in earthly time.

I am old enough now to look back on my life and declare the greatness of God, for the Lord has been my pathway. This was also David's declaration in 2 Samuel.

David typically concluded his military enterprises with a grateful review of all that God had done in the campaign. David took time to acknowledge in detail God's goodness and faithfulness. Unlike many of us who move through one difficulty after another, never pausing to declare God's wonderful deliverance, David was as careful to thank God for mercies, past and present, as to ask Him for future needs.

The Psalms are filled with David's songs of thanksgiving. But in 2 Samuel 22, we find David's grand hallelujah. In this psalm David, the warrior-king, reflects on what God has done in his life. David thanks God for the deliverances and good gifts of the past and then expresses unbounded confidence in God's mercy and goodness for the times to come.

David specifically praises God for His commands, which brought victory. At one point in the psalm, David claims that the successes he experienced were not because of his own abilities, but because he followed his heavenly Father's instructions.

The heroic exploits of David's men are also found in the concluding chapters of 2 Samuel. May this review of heroic acts and unbelievable feats summon us to realize the Lord's power within the impossibilities of our own lives.

Study Lesson 11

Daily Discovery I   **Heroic exploits**

1.   a.   Read 2 Samuel 21:15–22. We do not know the specific time period of the events in 2 Samuel 21:15–22.

b.   What does 2 Samuel 21:15–22 indicate about the type of men who served David? As you think of serving God, what does this suggest to you.

2.   Think through the truth set forth in 2 Timothy 3:16–17, and suggest several possible reasons why 2 Samuel 21:15–22 has been included in God's Word.

With Him in Life's Struggles

Daily Discovery II   **David's praise of God**

3. Studying David's Song of Thanksgiving will affect your life if you take time to reflect upon David's statements about God in 2 Samuel 22.

   a.   What strong pictures of God does David give us in 2 Samuel 22:2–3? Summarize the concept David is trying to communicate here.

   b.   In what way do these verses encourage you this week? Be specific.

4. a.   What types of difficulties does David state he often faced (2 Samuel 22:5–6, 17–19)?

   b.   Based on what David knows about God, what does he do in times of trouble (2 Samuel 22:2–7)? What is your first response to a difficulty? Having described at length the God who is strong enough to save him, David states for the record what has become his habitual exercise: "I call to the Lord" (22:4 and 22:7). This is a practice he shares with saints of all times and places (compare Job 27:10; Psalm 50:15; Isaiah 55:6; Lamentations 3:57; Romans 10:12; 1 Peter 1:17).

Daily Discovery III   **God responds to David**

5. a.   Briefly summarize God's response to David's cry for help (2 Samuel 22:7–17).

b. What are the implications concerning God's interest in your present situation? ". . . that God delights to give victory to his people to save/rescue them from all their enemies and from every calamity is a prominent thread running throughout the books of Samuel."[6]

c. What do the responses of God to His children teach us about our responses to those for whom we are responsible?

6. a. David gives testimony about his need and God's response. How would you describe this?

b. Since our God is "the same yesterday and today and forever" (Hebrews 13:8), what meaning does 2 Samuel 22:17–21 have for you in light of your present needs? "Just as calling to the Lord should be our lifelong response to an all-sufficient God (see vv. 2–3) who is worthy of praise (v. 4), so also calling to the Lord should be our immediate reaction (v. 7) when we are threatened by nameless dread or mortal danger. When in distress/trouble David and other afflicted saints know to whom to turn."[7]

c. Describe a time in which you were aware of the Lord's mighty working on your behalf (see Colossians 1:13–14 for one example).

Daily Discovery IV   **The possibility of blamelessness**

7.   a.   What is David able to say about his actions and attitudes in the past toward Saul (2 Samuel 22:21–25 along with the wise warnings found in 1 Samuel 25:23–31, especially verses 26, 28, 30–31)?

b.   David's declaration in vv. 21–25 can be understood as you work through the following comparison. Compare David's testimony (1 Samuel 26:23), the testimony of God (1 Kings 14:8), and the testimony of history (1 Kings 11:4; 15:5).

c.   As you consider your responses within your present circumstances, are you able to say what David says in 2 Samuel 22:22–24? Explain. How are you challenged here?

Daily Discovery V   **What God does for David**

8.   a.   What specific things did David remember about God as he faced difficult life situations (2 Samuel 22:29, 31)?

b.   What help do these verses offer you this week?

Lesson 11: Song of Thanksgiving

c.   When you are struggling to understand why things are happening as they are in your life, how would 2 Samuel 22:31 affect your perspective?

d.   If you make a decision to take refuge in God, what does He become to you in light of 2 Samuel 22:31? In what area of your life do you need to make this decision now?

9.   a.   Make a list of all that God has done for David. Use David's personal testimony in 2 Samuel 22:33–49 as your guide.

b.   Which of God's actions on behalf of David especially encourage you as you realize God can do the same in your life?

10. a.   Because of all God has done for David, what does David say he will do (2 Samuel 22:50)? What does this suggest to you personally?

b.   The apostle Paul makes this same declaration in the New Testament. Paul affirmed that the nations of the world would share in David's praise. (See Romans 15:9 which quotes 2 Samuel 22:50.) What personal application can you make here?

11. a.   In times of trouble David made the same decision as that encouraged in 1 Peter 4:19. What does this indicate in terms of your life?

b. In what ways does David's praise found in 2 Samuel 22 illustrate the wisdom of making such a decision?

c. How can sharing this truth with a child or a friend help them in their present situations? Give an example.

12. Take time today to look back over the ways the Lord has delivered you. List some of them here.

13. a. Discover five or more principles in David's song of praise for how you should live your life.

b. Take two of these principles and illustrate how you might apply them this week.

Key Principles from Lesson 11

1. We praise the Lord with thanksgiving when we specifically declare what He has done for us (2 Samuel 22).

2. We need to remind ourselves continually of what our God is like (2 Samuel 22:2–3). Then we will be encouraged to call upon God in faith (2 Samuel 22:4–7). For example, David reminded himself during difficulties that God was a rock, a fortress, a deliverer, a refuge, a stronghold, a shield (2 Samuel 22:2–3). Then he called upon the Lord for help (2 Samuel 22:4–7).

3. God responds to His children's cries for help (2 Samuel 22:7–17).

4. God's actions are directed to our specific points of need (2 Samuel 22:17–21).

5. As we appeal to God, we must also review our actions and attitudes (2 Samuel 22:22–24).

6. In any situation, coming to God lights our way (2 Samuel 22:29–31). When we question if what happened was right, remember: God's way is blameless, His word tested. We are "shielded" from evil when we make the decision to take refuge in God (2 Samuel 22:31–32).

7. When we first realize who God is and what He has done for us, and then remind ourselves of these truths, we will be motivated and encouraged to "commit [ourselves] to our faithful Creator and continue to do good" (1 Peter 4:19).

Lesson 12

A Morning Without Clouds

Memory Verse: "Therefore I will praise you, O LORD, among the nations; I will sing praises to your name" (2 Samuel 22:50).

It had been raining day after day. And now again it was raining as I sat at my desk studying David's last public words to his people. While I was studying, I was also struggling to accept a heartache in my life. Pensively I read those words spoken so long ago: "He [and his rule] is like the light of morning at sunrise on a cloudless morning, like the brightness after rain that brings the grass from the earth" (2 Samuel 23:4).

These were lovely words and a beautiful picture, yet somehow that day I could only see the rain.

The next morning as I awoke, I didn't hear the familiar sound of the rain. Walking outside, I was overwhelmed by the brilliance of the sunshine, the clearness of the sky. How fresh and radiant everything looked in the sparkling sunlight. Suddenly the words that I had pondered the day before began to make sense to me. This is what the rule of God is like in my life! When I'm submissive to His rule, the result is like the joyous beauty of this morning. Quietly, I submitted my heartache to His rule.

In this week's lesson, David's last words prophesy a glorious future hope. It is my desire that these words will be as relevant to you as they were to me.

Study Lesson 12

Daily Discovery I and II   **David's last words**

1.   How does David view himself at the close of his life? What observations do you make here (2 Samuel 23:1)?

2.   a.   As you read David's last message, who are you to recognize as the speaker (2 Samuel 23:2–3)?

    b.   How then, should you view these words?

    c.   What further insight do you get as you compare David's statement with that of the apostle Peter's in 2 Peter 1:21?

3.   a.   According to God, what two qualities are necessary for godly leadership (2 Samuel 23:3)?

    b.   What is such leadership like (2 Samuel 23:4)?

    c.   As you reflect on the word images God gives in 2 Samuel 23:4, what results can godly leadership produce in your life?

    d.   How can you relate these two aspects of godly leadership to any leadership positions you

With Him in Life's Struggles

have (as a mother, as a head of an organization or committee, as a teacher)?

4. To which ruler do David's words ultimately refer, according to Isaiah 11:1–5 and John 1:1–5, 14? What has been your own response to this ruler?

5. What covenant (agreement) had God previously made with David (2 Samuel 23:5; see also 2 Samuel 7:12, 16; Psalm 89:34–37)? How is this covenant described?

6. a. Why do you think this covenant is mentioned again? (Consider **who** is speaking, **when** he is speaking, and the **emphasis** of the message.)

b. What does David's assurance (2 Samuel 23:5) that God would keep His covenant indicate about his knowledge of God?

c. What significance is this covenant to us today (Isaiah 55:3–7)?

d. In light of these verses, have you become a part of this covenant? What does this mean concerning you?

7. a. What promise for the future is made in David's message (2 Samuel 23:3–5)?

b.   What warning is given (2 Samuel 23:6–7; see also Matthew 13:39–43)?

8.   a.   When God incorporates a list in His Word, it is for a reason. Why do you think God included the information found in this passage (2 Samuel 23:8–39)?

b.   As you reflect on this passage, what additional observations do you make?

Daily Discovery III   **The sinful command**

Though we don't know chronologically where to place the following important event, it probably took place late in David's reign. It was not, however, at the very close of his rule, even though it comes at the end of 2 Samuel. The kind of census described in this passage is one which a king would probably make during his years of strength.

9.   a.   Read 2 Samuel 24.

b.   How is the Lord described in 2 Samuel 24:1? The verse begins, "Again . . ." This also happened in 2 Samuel 21:1–2. What do you think is the root reason for this reaction?

c.   According to 1 Chronicles 21:1, who was the unseen instigator of this event?

d. What human being was used to effect evil (2 Samuel 24:1–2; 1 Chronicles 21:1–2)?

10. a. What command did David give in 2 Samuel 24:2?

b. From 2 Samuel 24:1–13, determine:

1) who first saw the command as sinful?

2) who next judged the command as sinful?

3) by whom it was finally seen as sinful?

11. a. In light of Joab's response to David (2 Samuel 24:3), what did David think would bring happiness?

b. What may have come into David's heart, allowing him to want to take a census?

c. What did Joab try to do about this situation?

d. Instead of giving David delight or pleasure, how did his actions affect him (2 Samuel 24:10, 12–17)? Do you think Joab was right in trying to stop David? Why or why not?

e. What application do you see here for your own life?

f. According to David himself in Psalm 30:6, what may have been the reason for David to think that he would "not be shaken"? (Notice also that both the 2 Samuel 24 and 1 Chronicles 21 account of this event are preceded by a list of military heroes.)

Daily Discovery IV   **Sin's effect**

12. a. What was David's clue that something was wrong (2 Samuel 24:10)?

b. What did David do about this clue?

c. Instead of this response, what other responses are often made in situations similar to the one described in 2 Samuel 24:10?

d. After a night of confession, what did David encounter in the morning (2 Samuel 24:11–13)?

e. What practical warning do you observe?

13. In light of 2 Samuel 24:14, what was David's reason for selecting the third judgment from the Lord? Do you think this was a wise conclusion? Why or why not?

14. a. How do the statements of the prophet Gad to David (2 Samuel 24:13), as well as what

took place in 2 Samuel 24:15, demonstrate that sin affects others?

b. Since numbers were so important to David, what may God have been trying to show him and the nation through this judgment?

c. What lesson or principle do you draw from this passage?

Daily Discovery V   **The plague is stopped**

15. a. What were David and Israel's elders doing while God's judgment fell on the nation (1 Chronicles 21:14–16)?

b. Express in your own words David's prayer (2 Samuel 24:17; 1 Chronicles 21:17)?

c. What characteristic revealed in David's prayer would you like to see in your own life?

16. a. Even before David's prayer, what had God's mercy already moved Him to do (2 Samuel 24:16)?

b. Even so, what was God's response to David's prayer (2 Samuel 24:18; 1 Chronicles 21:18)?

118

c. What was David's immediate action when God's Word was set before him (2 Samuel 24:18–20)?

17. a. In what ways does God go before and prepare Araunah's heart (1 Chronicles 21:18–23)?

b. How can this help you when God calls you to a particular task?

18. a. Describe David's attitude about his offerings to the Lord (2 Samuel 24:22–24).

b. What strong contrast to David's attitude is given in Malachi 1:11–14?

c. What has been your own attitude about your "offerings" to the Lord?

19. a. State the divine response that came as David offered his sacrifice before the Lord (2 Samuel 24:25; 1 Chronicles 21:26–28). How was the fire of the sacrifice kindled?

b. What future importance was this place of mercy to have (2 Chronicles 3:1)?

20. a. What did David conclude when God appeared above the threshing floor (1 Chronicles 21:26–22:1)?

b. In light of David's great desire expressed in 2 Samuel 7:2, why may this have been a time of particular joy to David? How did David express his joy (1 Chronicles 22:2–5)?

21. What kind of temple did David foresee? What was David's heart motive for such a magnificent temple (1 Chronicles 22:5)?

Key Principles from Lesson 12

1. We gain a healthy self-image when we view ourselves as God views us (2 Samuel 23:1).

2. When we read God's Word, we realize that the living God is speaking directly to us (2 Samuel 23:2–3).

3. According to God, two aspects of godly leadership are righteousness and reverence for God (2 Samuel 23:3).

4. Responding to godly leadership will bring peace, freshness, and light into our lives (2 Samuel 23:4).

5. The Righteous Ruler is Jesus Christ (Revelation 19:11–16).

6. God will always be faithful to His promises in His Word (2 Samuel 23:5–6; Psalm 89:3–4).

7.   Sin makes God angry (compare 2 Samuel 24:1 with 2 Samuel 21:1–2).

8.   When we choose not to walk in God's ways, we open ourselves up to being used by Satan for evil (2 Samuel 24).

9.   We need to take a stand against sin. To do so we must help each other (2 Samuel 24:3).

10. To take a proper stand against sin, we must know God's Word (2 Samuel 24:3).

11. It is important to be sensitive to God's warnings. We must listen when others question our actions in light of the Word (2 Samuel 24:3), and we must not ignore a troubled conscience (2 Samuel 24:10).

12. We cannot take sin lightly; sin has consequences (2 Samuel 24:11–15).

13. The wise are humble before God (1 Chronicles 21:14–16).

14. Even when we know God is going to punish us, it is wise to cast ourselves on His mercy (2 Samuel 24:14).

15. When God calls us to a work, He prepares a way for the task to be accomplished. If this involves others, He prepares their hearts (1 Chronicles 21:18–23).

16. Because the Lord is the great King, we should offer Him the best (2 Samuel 24:24; Malachi 1:13–14).

17. God's temple shows what God is like (1 Chronicles 22:5).

Lesson 13

The Charge

Memory Verse: "Observe what the LORD your God requires: Walk in his ways, and keep his decrees and commands, his laws and requirements, as written in the Law of Moses, so that you may prosper in all you do and wherever you go" (1 Kings 2:3).

The words "To our children, David, Christina, and Jonathan whom we pray will desire to be after God's heart" are written on the dedication page of *Loving and Obeying God,*[8] the Bible study book on 1 Samuel. The purpose of those words was not to look nice on the page, but to convey to our beloved children a message of great importance.

The Scripture declares, "The eyes of the LORD range throughout the earth to strengthen those whose hearts are fully committed to Him" (2 Chronicles 16:9). We want His eyes to see that our children's hearts are His. We want them to know His strong support in their lives.

Therefore, communicating the priority of knowing God and following in His ways is the most important thing we can do for them. And when this priority becomes their hearts' desire, then they will be after His heart.

My husband and I are not perfect at this job. We have had many good intentions that have failed. There have been times when our own sin has been in the way of accurately communicating what is involved in knowing God and following His ways. But God is powerful. Through the strength and wisdom of His Spirit we have had opportunity to demonstrate to our children in many practical ways the same important truth found in David's charge to his son: "Observe what the LORD your God requires: Walk in his ways, and keep his decrees and commands, his laws and requirements, as written in the Law of Moses, so that you may prosper in all you do and wherever you go" (1 Kings 2:3). David wanted Solomon to succeed, and he knew that the only route was to follow God's ways. Before Solomon could follow God's ways, he had to know them. David, therefore, stressed the priority of God's Word to his son. My husband and I have seen the result of this priority in our own children's lives.

David teaches us a key lesson through his challenge to Solomon. When we personally respond to David's message, our children (and others) witness the good effect of God's truth in our lives. In turn they will be encouraged to live life God's way.

Study Lesson 13

Daily Discovery I **The final crisis in David's life**

1. Read 1 Kings 1.
2. Cultural note on 1 Kings 1:1–4: Medical science in David's time held that warmth was brought to the aged by the body of another human being. That the body heat be from a young and beautiful human being was no doubt an extra, even in David's culture.

3. a. Even in his old age, David faced problems within his household. What two ideas conveyed in 1 Kings 1:5–6 indicate the lifestyle of David's son Adonijah? How may Adonijah's lifestyle have influenced his actions in 1 Kings 1:7–10, 25–26?

b. What personal observations can you draw from these passages?

4. Name the key people in David's government who Adonijah was able to ask for help (1 Kings 1:7). Who remained faithful to David (1 Kings 1:8)?

5. a. As David begins to approach the difficult issue that Nathan the prophet presents to him, of what important fact is David reminded (1 Kings 1:29)?

b. How did this truth encourage David, as well as those to whom he spoke?

c. Apply this principle to your own life.

6. a. Carefully study 1 Kings 1:10–48 to determine how Adonijah was stopped. Record your observations here.

b. What do you learn about God from this event? Where possible, support your conclusions from the passage, listing the specific verses.

7. Describe some of the end results in the lives of the people who chose not to do things God's way (1 Kings 1:49–53).

Daily Discovery II **David's charge to his son**

8. a. What is David's greatest concern in his final charge to Solomon (1 Kings 2:1–4)?

b. What does this concern indicate about David's heart attitude toward God and his ways?

c. If you have a child (or close friend), what is your greatest concern for him or her? What specifically are you doing about it?

9. a. What great project was Solomon called to do? Who called him to the task (1 Chronicles 22:6–11)?

b. What did David know about his son Solomon (1 Chronicles 22:5)?

c. Carefully study 1 Chronicles 22:5–17. Knowing his son's need, determine at least five ways in which David prepared Solomon for the future, particularly in regard to Solomon's special calling.

d. What principles did David state would secure genuine prosperity for his son (1 Chronicles 22:12–13)? Think of at least one practical way in which you can convey this same truth to your child (or friend).

10. a. According to 1 Chronicles 22:12–13 what two qualities did David desire for his son? Why were these qualities necessary for Solomon? Why would they be necessary for you in your current life situations and responsibilities? Give a specific example.

b. David's statements must have affected Solomon. What did Solomon ask of the Lord in 1 Kings 3:7–10?

c. How did the Lord respond to Solomon's request (1 Kings 3:10–14)?

11. a. Though Solomon was to take the lead in the great task the Lord had set before him, who was to help him (1 Chronicles 22:17–19)?

b. What key statement does David make in 1 Chronicles 22:18 that would be strong encouragement to a leader of Israel? What did the Lord do to make it possible for time to be given to the work?

c. What heart attitude was to accompany the labor (1 Chronicles 22:19)?

d. Write out an application of this principle for an area of your life.

Daily Discovery III   **David's address concerning the temple**

12. a   Read 1 Chronicles 28.
    b.   Who drew up the plans for the majestic Solomonic temple? What does this public address reveal to you about David and about God?

Daily Discovery IV   **Sacrificial offering for the temple**

13. a.   Read 1 Chronicles 29.
    b.   What had the people seen modeled for them that helped them understand how to give (1 Chronicles 29:2–5, 9).

    c.   What was particularly important about the offerings that were made for the temple (1 Chronicles 29:1–9, 14–17)?

    d. How does this concept change your own personal worship?

Daily Discovery V   **David's final prayer**

14. In 1 Chronicles 29:10–19 we read the last public prayer of one who walked with God. What do you learn about prayer from David?

15. Using David's prayer as a source, develop at least five principles about how you should live.

Key Principles from Lesson 13

1. Remembering the powerful deeds of God in our lives encourages us in present difficulties (1 Kings 1:29).

2. The purposes of God cannot be thwarted (1 Kings and 1 Chronicles 22:9–10).

3. Walking in God's ways brings godly success (1 Kings 2:3 and 1 Chronicles 22:13).

4. We need discernment and understanding to apply God's word to our daily lives (1 Chronicles 22:12).

5. It is pleasing to the Lord when we ask Him for the ability to discern between good and evil (1 Kings 3:9–10).

6. It is God who commissions us to do tasks for Him (1 Chronicles 22:10).

7. It is wise to set our heart and soul to seek the Lord in any leadership role, or work we are called to by God (1 Chronicles 22:19).

8. Willingly offering back to God with a whole heart that which He has given brings us joy (1 Chronicles 29:9, 14).

Notes

[1] J. Sidlow Baxter, *Explore the Book* (Grand Rapids: Zondervan Publishing House, 1960), 70.

[2] Most scholars believe that the "River of Egypt" is the Wadi el-Arish.

[3] Derek Kidner, *Psalms 1–72*, (Leicester: InterVarsity Press, 1973), 215.

[4] Dr. Harry Johnson, *Executive Lifestyles*, cited by Andrew B. Seidel in the sermon "David and Bathsheba" delivered at the International Chapel of Vienna, March 6, 1994.

[5] Ronald F. Youngblood, "II Samuel," in Frank E. Gaebelein, ed., *The Expositor's Bible Commentary, Vol. 3*, (Grand Rapids: Zondervan, 1991), 1048, citing Walter Brueggeman, *First and Second Samuel*, 332.

[6] *Ibid.*, 1067.

[7] *Ibid.*, 1068.

[8] Myrna Alexander, *Loving and Obeying God* (Grand Rapids: Zondervan, 1982). *Loving and Obeying God* was formally called *After God's Heart*.

Note to the Reader

The publisher invites you to share your response to the message of this book by writing Discovery House Publishers, Box 3566, Grand Rapids, MI 49501, USA. For information about other Discovery House books, music, or videos, contact us at the same address or call 1-800-653-8333. Find us on the Internet at http://www.dhp.org/ or send e-mail to books@dhp.org.